M000106893

Also By Christine Kloser

A DAILY DOSE OF LOVE
Everyday Inspiration to Help You Remember
What Your Heart Already Knows

PEBBLES IN THE POND
Transforming the World One Person at a Time
(Wave One)

PEBBLES IN THE POND
Transforming the World One Person at a Time
(Wave Two)

PEBBLES IN THE POND
Transforming the World One Person at a Time
(Wave Three)

PEBBLES IN THE POND
Transforming the World One Person at a Time
(Wave Four)

CONSCIOUS ENTREPRENEURS
A Radical New Approach to Purpose, Passion and Profit

THE FREEDOM FORMULA
How to Put Soul in Your Business
and Money in Your Bank

INSPIRATION TO REALIZATION
Real Women Reveal Proven Strategies for Personal,
Business, Financial and Spiritual Fulfillment

PEBBLES

in the

POND

*Transforming the World
One Person at a Time*

~Wave Five~

Transformation Books
York, PA

Pebbles in the Pond: Transforming the World One Person at a Time (Wave Five)

Published by:
Transformation Books
211 Pauline Drive #513
York, PA 17402
www.TransformationBooks.com

ISBN: 978-1-945252-00-6

Cover design by Sarah Barrie
Layout and typesetting by Ranilo Cabo
Editor: Marlene Oulton, *www.MarleneOulton.com*
Editor: Gwen Hoffnagle, *www.GwenHoffnagle.com*
Printed in the United States of America

Help Me Be...

Strong enough to be vulnerable.

Wise enough to realize how little I know.

Loving enough to embrace my "enemy."

Tender enough to be powerful.

Smart enough to realize I can't do it alone.

Brilliant enough to shine the light of others.

Doubtful enough to know the power of faith.

Courageous enough to share my truth.

~ Christine Kloser

Table of Contents

Introduction

"A small body of determined spirits fired by an unquenchable faith in their mission can alter the course of history."

~ Gandhi

THANK YOU FOR FOLLOWING THE WHISPER in your heart to pick up this book and crack open the cover. My guess is — like the contributors to this book — you've been on a powerful, transformational journey that sometimes joyously surprises you and other times throws you an unexpected curve ball that knocks you to your knees.

Perhaps as you read this you're in the middle of the most challenging time of your life. Or maybe you've just come through a difficult situation with a renewed sense of faith and hope. Perhaps you have a niggling sense that a growth opportunity is lurking around the corner waiting for you, but you just don't know what it is… yet.

No matter where you stand right now on your path, I trust that since you're here — taking time to read this book — you believe in the concept of a "pebble in the pond" and share in the vision of a world that is transformed one person at a time.

While world transformation may seem like a far-fetched dream, the truth I've come to know is that as we transform as individuals, we *do* make a difference in the lives of those around us. And if you've ever thrown a stone in a still pond, you know that one single splash sends

1

ripples outward in every direction, creating more and more ripples. It's the same thing when that "splash" is the impact of your life and how you live it each and every day — the impact expands.

It doesn't matter if you're a leading-edge entrepreneur, schoolteacher, mom, rocket scientist, doctor, writer, healer, manager, salesperson, nurse, volunteer, retiree, or anything else; your life — and how you live it — can be a force for good in our world. Every person has the power to make a difference, including you, and that's exactly what this book is about.

At this time in history we are on the precipice of experiencing the new world many people have been dreaming about — a world filled with love, cooperation, contribution, service, community, and abundance for all. And there are a growing number of people who are doing all they can to heal themselves, become a part of the solution (simply by being who they truly and authentically are), and bring more light and love into the world.

In the pages of this book you'll meet such visionary leaders and world-changers. You might recognize some of the contributors as leaders in the world. Others aren't as well known, yet their stories are testaments to the power of one person's transformational journey to send ripples of good into the world.

I personally feel so blessed to receive the gift of working closely with the contributors to this book. We've gathered together over the course of eight months to birth this book in service to you. As you discover each contributor's story, you'll see why I consider it a blessing to call them my clients, soul travelers, and friends. *Pebbles in the Pond — Wave Five* is only possible because of the love and light they bring to the world.

Some chapters will make you cry, while others will make you laugh. Some will touch your heart deeply, while others will inspire you to think differently. Some chapters will be difficult to read as you hear of the challenges a few of the authors have faced that nobody should ever have to live through. And others will offer you a heartfelt reassurance

2

that if they can do it (whatever the "it" is), you can, too. Also, as you read through this book I invite you to embrace the great diversity of the contributing authors. Their ethnicities, religious beliefs, career paths, backgrounds, and journeys are as diverse as can be. Yet, as you will see on the pages, their hearts all stand for the same thing... unity, peace and love. So allow yourself to perhaps be stretched and expanded into seeing another's point of view. I assure you that if the entire world population had the depth of acceptance and appreciation these authors have for each other – in all their diversity – the world truly would experience peace on earth.

So as you proceed through this book, don't feel the need to read the chapters in order. Chances are as you peruse the table of contents or randomly flip open the pages, you will receive exactly the message that is meant for you in that moment.

Above all else, let the stories in this book bathe you in love, compassion, understanding, and inspiration to transform your challenges and struggles (large or small) into beautiful blessings for yourself and others.

You never know what miracle may happen as a result of reading one of these stories. In fact, this book series in and of itself is evidence of the miraculous grace that appeared during the most challenging time of my life. In the first "wave" of *Pebbles in the Pond* (published in 2012), the title of my chapter was "The Best 'Worst' Time of My Life."

It was the worst time because I was going through personal bankruptcy and a very challenging dissolution of a business partnership, unsure about how I was going to support my family and questioning everything about who I knew myself to be. Saying I felt like a failure puts it mildly. Yet that challenging time opened my heart in ways I never knew possible – and one of the many "gifts in the challenge" was the concept for this book series.

With this – Wave Five of *Pebbles in the Pond* – the ripples continue to encompass and empower you to be who you are here to be... and to let your light shine!

On behalf of myself and all of the contributing authors of this series, we send you our deepest blessings that this book delivers the inspiration and transformation your soul is seeking. May you be guided by grace.

Love and blessings,
Christine Kloser,
The Transformation Catalyst®

Soulful and Successful

Christine Kloser

IN 2011, WHEN I WAS AT THE LOWEST POINT of my life going through bankruptcy and foreclosure, I never could have imagined where I'd be now in 2016. My journey has had many twists and turns, high points, and great challenges over the past five years. One of the greatest challenges I've faced lately is learning how to love myself enough to say yes to myself and my business instead of sacrificing what is right for my soul's journey out of fear of hurting other people's feelings and not being liked.

I had to make some very difficult decisions over the past year, some that were quite painful even though they were for the best. I had to let go of expectations, old beliefs, and how I thought it "should" be, and instead be at peace right where I am on the journey... without regret, fear, putting others' needs before my own, or keeping my mouth shut in order to not rock the boat.

There's no way for me to describe this shift and transformation within me other than to state that it was a nudge from my soul. Deep down inside I knew change was coming, and as much as I wanted to avoid it, it kept bubbling up until it was undeniable and life demanded that I make a big change.

Maybe you've had similar experiences, where you were resistant or scared to do something out of fear but you couldn't deny that something was happening, forcing you to take the next step while giving you the courage you needed and the confidence to take that perhaps dreaded action that was for your highest good.

It is moments like these that I believe define us. Do we choose to stay scared, timid, hidden, and safe, or do we allow that nudge from our soul to guide us, and trust it no matter what?

This was the question I asked while I was on my knees filled with so much fear, pain, and self-doubt around the time of my bankruptcy. It didn't matter how terrified I was at that time. Something inside drove me to ask the difficult questions of myself and of God, wait and listen for the answers, and then have the courage to act despite my external circumstances.

That inner knowing, let's call it my soul's calling, wouldn't let me off the hook. It demanded more of me. It demanded that I not curl up and spend the rest of my life under a rock. It demanded I serve from what I learned. And serve I did!

From 2011 to 2016, following those nudges from my soul, I facilitated training for nearly 70,000 aspiring transformational authors and messengers from more than 100 countries. I developed several new programs, held live events and retreats, and grew my business past the million-dollar mark. I don't share this to impress you, but rather to stress the importance and value of listening to those nudges from your soul. They are signposts from the Universe as to the next steps to take, and are well worth your time, focus, and attention. This is not to say that following your nudges will lead you down the same path I was led, but I am saying that following *your* nudges will lead *you* to exactly where you are meant to be.

One example of this is that soon after making some big (and difficult) decisions in my business, I crossed paths with the most perfect person I could ever imagine to help me move my business forward from here. Actually, this person was beyond the biggest dream I had in terms of support for my business.

Interestingly enough, I barely made it to the meeting where we crossed paths because I was nearly stranded by a blizzard. But when something is written in the soul's plan, heaven and earth conspire for it to happen as long as you pay attention, follow your nudges, and take action.

As I was talking with this new friend, he struggled to figure out how I've achieved the success I've had over the past five years. And in all honestly, I do not have any clear, concise strategy or plan for how it happened. My "strategy" was to pay attention, listen to my intuition, work on myself, stay committed to my personal/spiritual growth, and take inspired action when guided to do so. That is not much of a strategy in traditional business terms, but it has worked well for me.

Now I am faced with a new challenge as a result of the past five years: to try to reverse-engineer how I did what I did. I'm being nudged to do this work because of the immense pain I see in people who keep trying and trying to be "successful"... but it's not working. I have spoken with many people who achieved what they perceived as success, only to have them confide in me that they were miserable and felt something was missing in their life. Their material success felt empty, and in many cases made things worse.

My journey has been one in which my business and my life work in tandem. I take good care of my body, mind, and soul, have a wonderful marriage, enjoy being a mother, embrace precious time with my family as the gift it is, and have good friends and a lot of great support in my life. This is what I want for everyone. So of course my soul is pressing on me (it has been since early 2014) to do the work to figure out what has made my journey possible so I can provide insight, inspiration, and action steps for people who want so much more than what they have, yet don't know how to make it their reality.

Before I share what I've learned about being *Soulful and Successful*®, I first want to address what I mean by "success" and the desire for "more." The "success" and the "more" I'm referring to are not about amassing more money, more fame, more toys, more gadgets, more accumulation of anything materialistic, though for many these things become by-products of living a *Soulful and Successful* life. Rather, what I'm referring to is that deeper desire for more — more expression, more love, more fulfillment, more joy, more abundance (which also includes money), and more peace, to name a few. This is the "more," the "success" that speaks to the soul. It is the impulse within you that goes back to the inception of life itself that wants to be expressed through you.

In my opinion the word *success* needs global redefinition, because the pursuit of success (using the current mass-consciousness meaning) has brought more pain, control, fear, depression, anxiety, separation, terror, and hopelessness than the world has ever seen. Something has to change from the top to the bottom and the bottom to the top, from politics, corporate conglomerates, and our education systems to home, family, and our own individual hearts.

We cannot wait for change to come from the top down. The entirety of the Universe is begging us as human beings on planet Earth at this time to bring our highest selves into the world, knowing that as we discover and live our souls' callings we are fulfilling our pieces of the cosmic puzzle and contributing to a global shift of consciousness.

You may think I've lost my marbles and that the shift to a "new world" will never happen. But I assure you, it is possible and it is happening. There is more evidence than ever, perhaps even more than all the negativity that runs rampant in the media, that there is *good* in the world, and we are firmly on our way to a new and much more joyous and peaceful human experience.

I believe this shift will happen when we all redefine success for ourselves and pursue it with every part of our bodies, our minds, and most especially, our souls. This is why the Universe has nudged me out of my comfort zone to look at how I've done what I've done, bucking the norm and doing what's right for me along the way. I keep feeling that deep calling that says *this* is the new way for us to be in the world.

Just imagine what it would be like if every human being on the planet were guided by their soul – the pure essence of who they are that is directly connected to All that exists in the Universe – and if every human being pursued a success that wasn't about accumulation of assets and power, but accumulation of love, joy, fulfillment, contribution, and true human connection. We, as a species, would stand in awe at the miracles and grace that unfold when we do this.

This has been my journey for the past five years from bankrupt to seven-figure CEO of a company that has brought love, joy, fulfillment, and my contribution and connection to tens of thousands of people around the world. I hope you see that my material success was not my focus, but the by product of my *Soulful and Successful* path.

Before I wrap this up, I want to offer you five key questions that, when answered, will help you set foot on *your Soulful and Successful* path, too. Your path will not look like mine because your *unique* path is already perfectly laid out for you... and your soul is calling you to take the next step on it. Otherwise your soul wouldn't have led you to this moment, right now, in which you are reading about this very thing. Your soul knows what you need! I trust you're paying attention now.

I strongly encourage you to grab your journal, write down these questions, and write your answers by the end of the day.

Five Key Questions for a *Soulful and Successful* Life

1. Is there an area of your life (family, health, relationship, career, etc.) in which you feel a nudge from your soul for something "more?" If so, which area, and what is the nudge asking of you?

2. What is your personal definition of success? (Be careful that society's norm doesn't influence your answer. This is about you!)

3. When you experience that success, how will the world (in your own backyard or around the globe) be better as a result?

4. What, if any, old beliefs or fears do you want to release in order to open more to pursuing the path of your soul?

5. Given all you've discovered in this process, what is one concrete action you can take immediately to take a step on your *Soulful and Successful* path?

Don't let the soul-nudge you're feeling right now go unnoticed. If you read this entire chapter right up to these very words, I trust it is because you were meant to receive this message. There is a gift for you here and now when you listen to that nudge and work through these questions.

I hope you're paying attention...

Known to many as "The Transformation Catalyst®," **Christine Kloser** is a respected leader, speaker, author, coach, and mentor. Since 2007 she has been on a mission to help aspiring authors liberate their soul's message and bring it forth in the world. She is thrilled to expand her work and help transform the world one person at a time by teaching people how to live a *Soulful and Successful* life. Discover how Christine can help you take the next step on your Soulful and Successful journey at www.ChristineKloser.com and www.SoulfulAndSuccessful.com.

The Uncomfortable Zone: The Bumpy Journey to What Is Possible

Don Awalt

I WALKED OUT OF BANKRUPTCY COURT, paused on the steps, and looked up into the sky. I felt naked, with everything stripped away. I was alone. I had no one to call. I felt hopeless, defeated, lonely... and simply drained. My biggest concern was not the lack of money, bank accounts, or credit, but how to keep this a secret. I was a fool to think that I could hide my pain. Those closest to me knew something was going on, but I had built up such a high wall of fear that it kept them out. Otherwise, they might come to know the truth: that I wasn't the intelligent, confident, and successful person with tremendous potential they thought I was... or at least, what *I thought they thought*.

But on that day I turned my gaze upwards, peering through the tall buildings surrounding the courthouse. There was nowhere left to hide. It was a pleasant autumn day, with puffy clouds dotting a brilliant blue sky. The air was brisk. A few birds darted between the trees and buildings. In spite of what I'd experienced, I took gratitude in the beauty around me. Frankly, it was all I could do because my mind could not grasp the magnitude of what had just happened. While part of me said, "All is in order; things happen for a reason," another voice was screaming, "You fool. You could have prevented this!" I was in a state where denial and reality met. In a solemn daze I thought, "Okay, that's behind me. Now what?"

This was not the most traumatic event of my life, and I know there are people who have been through far worse. But this blow took me down hard. I was nearly fifty years old, and now broke. My career was that of a financial advisor. I had dreams and aspirations of making a difference in the lives of others, and had been amply rewarded for my efforts. But I was living a delusional irony: advising others about money when I could not manage my own. I had stubbornly pursued this work, building my own business to prove to myself and others that I could make it work. It all crumbled around me as I came to accept I was doing something that didn't really resonate with me. I quietly picked up the remaining pieces of my shattered life and hoped no one would find out about this appalling experience I'd just gone through.

In the difficult months that followed, I was fortunate enough to return to a full-time job that paid very well and where my contribution was appreciated. It was there I stayed for quite a while, hiding in shame. I had to accept defeat, paying the bills that were not relieved by bankruptcy and managing to save a bit of money. But the steady paycheck and benefits I received were not fulfilling, and I had no idea what I was going to do next. I was very unsettled. And though I did my best to hide it, I was not happy.

I was in what I came to call the Uncomfortable Zone, where the dissatisfaction of the current situation meets the indecision of what to do about it. It was this event that made me realize I knew this place very well. In some form or another I had lived most of my life in the Uncomfortable Zone – not satisfied, but fearful of making a change.

I knew I wasn't alone. The work I did as an advisor led me into the homes and sitting at the kitchen table with many couples. The tension of talking about money gripped our conversations. And it was evident to me that this tension carried over into their relationships. Those who were having a difficult time dealing with debt that overshadowed their savings knew they needed to make a change, yet were very anxious about doing so. Very few ever mentioned being satisfied with their work or having purpose in what they did. And it seemed that this general dissatisfaction was not limited to money and the effect it has on relationships. Research shows that most people are unhappy about some aspect of their life – money, work, marriage, family, health issues, etc. – and many struggle with depression.

If you can relate to this uneasiness, feeling as if your life could be better yet at a loss to do anything about it, you, too, know the Uncomfortable Zone. It can be a prison where you learn to settle for what you have and do what you can to be happy. Unfortunately it is where many people stay, paralyzed with indecision and fearful of making a change. And it is unlikely you will ever go back to being perfectly comfortable with what had been. The reminder that you *"could have, should have, and probably would have... only if... but..."* leaves you unsettled.

As I approached the half-century point of my life, I experienced a cold awakening that I was adopting this sense of regret for what could have been. I realized that if I did not make some changes I would stay imprisoned within myself, just like many others, complacent with settling for less than I deserved. I knew there was something better, but I was unclear about what that was. I didn't know what I wanted to do with my career, what I wanted in a relationship, where I wanted to live, or even how I wanted to live. And when a twinkling of a dream crept in that someday things might get better, it was immediately sabotaged with the belief that I couldn't have it or didn't deserve it. I was hesitant to talk to anyone about it because I wanted to keep my secret and pretend that everything was just fine.

In the months following the bankruptcy, I made feeble attempts to lift myself out from under the muck and mire of depression, suppressing my feelings by being quietly in denial. I understood that it was important to be in gratitude for what I did have, yet this only served to mask the dissatisfaction with my life and allow fear to hold me back from taking any steps forward. I could only be grateful for so long.

I tried to think in better terms and be positive. Doubt would set in and faith would erode into skepticism and pessimism. I took caution in the choices I made, minimizing risk as much as possible. I pretended to make desirable things that weren't. I knew it was possible to change, that there was something better; and in many cases I even knew what I needed to do... I just didn't feel I could do it. And it kept coming back to haunt me. I wasn't happy with my job, I wasn't happy about my health, loving relationships eluded me, and financially I was a wreck. It seemed a monumental task to turn all of this around. So I remained in the prison cell of my Uncomfortable Zone... quiet, covert, and alone. I was secretly beating myself up one moment, and in the next wanting something much greater. I was caught in an internal battle, having desires without the courage to pursue them.

I finally discerned that there were only two options: stay dissatisfied and complacent with things the way they were *or* make a change. I was standing at a fork in the road. In one direction was "Survival Road" where I could keep doing what I had been, knowing deep inside that I could get by, yet hoping for some miracle. This road was familiar and predictable. I knew I could navigate it and exist, though I didn't like that option. It wouldn't lead me to where I wanted to go. In the other direction was the "Unknown Way," full of mystery and fear of the unknown. What would I do? What if I found I wasn't happy with my choices? What if I failed again and things ended up even worse?

I came to realize that the Uncomfortable Zone begins when we reach this crossroad. There is dissatisfaction in the direction we are going and doubt that things will ever get better. Yet changing direction does not take us out of the Zone. It is uncomfortable to overcome the beliefs we hold from past history — the self-doubt, the influence others have on us, and the evidence we have to support being cautious. There was one and only one thought that gave me the courage to not give in to my fears: "Others have done it, so why not me?"

When I decided to make a change, there were many setbacks. I faced obstacles with money, managing my time, and believing in myself. I knew I needed time to write my books and develop my products, but each day I juggled self-doubt and hope. I was still dependent on my paycheck, and I wondered if I could meet and exceed my current income, and how I could do that. I struggled with the thought of giving up and staying on the "Survival Road." I have seen many get trapped in this cycle, in which they try something new, get pushed back, give up, and settle with being dissatisfied. And this is where I had been most of my life, until it came to me: *"When the benefits of making a change outweigh the benefits of being complacent, change takes place."*

The bankruptcy papers in my hand, evidence of an ill-fated attempt to change, had been justification for me to be complacent. Yet I could not use this setback as another excuse to do nothing. I made the decision that I was going to continue to try, but this time around in a responsible way. It looked likely that I would be working most of the rest of my life. Being broke at almost fifty, retirement didn't seem to be much of an option. So if I was going to be working for many years, I'd better do something I loved.

I spent a couple of years in personal introspection. I became aware of how I showed up in the world. I learned to accept myself as perfectly imperfect, and to be who I am with both my strengths and my weaknesses. In seeking a new path, I found I didn't need to make big changes, just little course corrections. I felt it was only a matter of adjusting my attitude, staying clear about what I wanted, and consistently doing *something* to actively pursue my dreams. It was difficult to do so amid all the disparaging and negative thoughts that continued to reside in my head, but I nurtured myself with positive influences and shielded myself from the negative.

In time I began to trust my intuition. I monitored my thoughts, catching the doubtful, discouraging feelings and repackaging them as reminders to move with responsibility. I began to ask for help from those around me. I spent time studying myself and becoming aware of

15

how I was thinking. And though I had difficulty dealing with what I had been through, I cautiously invested money in personal development courses and coaches.

As I now pursue my work, I remind myself that the objective is to have fun and make my work something I want to do. Instead of working to create my life, I now live to create my work. I know it is natural to slip into the Uncomfortable Zone when I have occasional feelings of self-doubt, frustration, and indecision, or experience events that stir fear in what I am doing. I admit there are times when I am ready to give up and just settle for the way it is. Yet I now welcome these feelings as guideposts moving me to live in a more accountable way.

I continue to move forward, inspired by the meaningful and valuable work I do. While taking the steps down this new path, I remember to stop often, look up to the sky, feel the essence of creation all around me, and take in the magnificence of life and each of our divine parts in it. I remind myself of what I have accomplished, the tasks I have completed, and the changes I have made within. I give thanks, and with eager anticipation I ponder the thought, "Okay, that's behind me. Now what?"

Don Awalt, an accomplished musician, a single father of three adult children, and an avid student of personal and professional development, has spent most of his career in corporate America. His passion is helping people through personal transformation and working with companies to create an environment of meaningful work for their employees. His book, *The Uncomfortable Zone,* will be released in 2016. Visit TheUncomfortableZone.com for more information and a complementary study guide.

Heart Gifts of HOPE

"Bea" Joy Christianna Baldoz

IT WAS THE WORST AND THE BEST YEAR EVER. Some say it was my *season of serendipity*, but I'm delighted to call it my *season of sweet Divinity*, during which I experienced God's loving generosity. I had already surrendered my heart to God's call on my life, but the Spirit within me knew fears and doubts stood in my way. My faith needed to be strengthened and my heart refined through circumstances that would come to test me. That season became a turning point in my transformational journey that gave light to my true heart's calling. I had longed for confirmations and discovered that God was delighted to give them to me while demonstrating His presence, power, and love. It's truly an honor and privilege to be able to share with you the story of my worst and best season – a season when God allowed difficult circumstances to draw me closer to His heart and His purposes, plans, and precious promises for me, all on a path filled with *heart gifts of HOPE*.

Milestones and Emotions

In 2013, my husband and I joyously celebrated our twentieth wedding anniversary, and our daughters turned sixteen and thirteen. Together we had experienced many joys and sorrows in the span of two decades, but 2013 was definitely the year my family would endure extremely difficult circumstances. My beloved father passed away unexpectedly in March of that year; I was physically assaulted at my father's funeral reception; and my family was deeply wounded by betrayals of people we never expected would betray us. Hearts heavy, we pursued a necessary protective restraining order in light of threats made by my assailant. And while we received a favorable ruling following six months of heart-wrenching court hearings, the negative impact of the assault itself was not easy to shake off.

I was in a state of shock for some time after the attack. Eventually I was diagnosed with symptoms of post-traumatic stress disorder. But God, according to His promise in Romans 8:28 (NIV), who works "… all things together for good to those who love him and are called according to his purpose," strengthened and blessed us in the midst of our painful circumstances and worked out many miracles — more than I am able to share in this chapter.

The Miracle of the Job Offer

On a Sunday evening, three days after the assault, my husband gathered us together for a family meeting to share some happy news. I felt a sense of relief upon hearing him announce that he had received, on the same day as my father's funeral, notification of a new job offer, and that he had plans to accept it.

Monday morning, the next day, the assault replayed in my mind at the same time I was grieving the loss of my dad. I was distraught, hurting emotionally and physically. I couldn't hold back tears while silently praying to God that I'd hear my husband say "I'm taking a day off from work to comfort you." He didn't say that. He had to go work. His plan that morning was to give two weeks' notice to his current employer, finish strong, and then be set to start his new job.

However, before he even had a chance to give his notice, he was called in for a meeting and informed that he was immediately being laid off… with severance! He no longer *needed* to give his two-week notice. We were glad to be home together for the next two weeks. For these abundant blessings, we continually give praise to Almighty God, "…who is able," according to the Scriptures, "to do immeasurably more than all we ask or imagine according to his power that is at work within us." (Ephesians 3:20 NIV)

The Basket Blessing and Messages to Run My Race

Two months after the assault, I almost skipped a "Moms in Prayer" celebration brunch due to feeling depressed, but the Spirit within me battled and conquered negative thoughts that were trying to convince me to just stay in bed. Thankfully I ended up attending. During the brunch I was the winner of a coffee-themed prize basket. I was delighted, for it was a cute, miniature replica of a special basket I once owned and had been sorry to lose. My own basket had gone missing during my father's viewing at the funeral home.

Among the coffee-related items in the prize basket was a handwritten note that said, "Dear Prayer Warrior Mom, You have been running your race for a while… but you're not finished yet… keep running." I was moved as I read that note. Just hours before I had wept on my pillow and cried out, "God, I'm so weary. I can't run this race any longer… please help me!" I'm grateful He responded by giving me the strength to attend the brunch and by providing me encouragement through the basket blessing.

Two months later, also in answer to prayers, I received word from the Billy Graham Training Center (BGTC) in Asheville, North Carolina, that I had been granted a full scholarship to attend a seminar from July 15th to 19th entitled "When God Says, '*Well Done!*' – Running the Race to Win the Prize." This was intensive spiritual training – an in-depth study of the book of Hebrews. The Spirit that dwells in me knew this would give me strength to keep running my race.

Honey from The Rock

During the arrival dinner at BGTC on July 14th, a pastor on staff, cousin of world-famous evangelist Reverend Billy Graham, shared a devotional message titled "Honey from The Rock." The pastor said things such as "The greater one's suffering, the greater one's anointing," and "Trials have a beginning and end; and blessings will come out of the hardest circumstances we face."

The pastor referred to the blessings that come out of hardships as "Honey from The Rock," and referred to God as "The Rock." I found the message difficult to fully embrace in that moment, as fiery darts of doubt came against me in rapid-fire fashion.

A Heart-Shaped Rock

The next morning, July 15th, I had some free time and went hiking on a beautiful mountain trail that leads to the top of The Overlook at The Cove, located on the majestic grounds of BGTC. While on the solo hike, I took some time to sit on a rock and pray. Sobbing, I expressed aloud how my heart felt so broken. I discussed with God my doubts about any kind of anointing over me and that anything sweet like honey could come out of my circumstances. But I felt led to ask, "Please help me believe that blessings, or 'honey from The Rock,' will come after enduring these hardships. Please help me remember this somehow." As I looked toward the rocky path before me, tears streaming down my face, I made this request: "To help me remember, will you please let me have a heart-shaped rock? And can it be white?" I was surprised by my request for a white, heart-shaped rock, but the request had flowed straight out of my broken heart.

Less than five minutes after saying that prayer, and while taking steps forward on that mountainside path covered by a myriad of rocks, I spied a white rock slightly covered in dirt that resembled a heart. I immediately picked it up, brushed off the dirt, and there appeared on it a line that looked like a crack. The rock resembled a fractured heart. It even had a little chip in it as well. It immediately reminded me of my own broken heart. I then flipped the rock over to the other side and exclaimed, "Whoa!" That side was smooth and whole, resembling a completely healed heart. What amazed me even more was that it had the outline of a finger on it. Upon seeing that, God's Spirit brought to my remembrance this Scripture promise: "Trust in The Lord with all your heart; lean not on your own understanding, acknowledge Him in all your ways and He will direct your path." (Proverbs 3:5-6 NIV) The rock and this precious promise were *heart gifts of HOPE* from God's loving heart to mine. I felt moved to re-surrender and acknowledge that God rules, reigns, and guides me on His chosen path for me, as I trust in Him.

The Little Town that Rocks

When the seminar at BGTC concluded, I made plans for a mini writing retreat before heading to Charlotte to attend "She Speaks," a writer-speaker conference. The retreat was at the home of a woman who owns a cozy cottage in Candler, North Carolina. On Monday, July 22nd, the final day of my mini-retreat, I decided to write a poem atop Mount Mitchell, the highest mountain east of the Mississippi River. I embarked on an adventurous journey to this mountaintop and was grateful to be able to write my desired poem titled "Who Is Like God?" which is what the name Mitchell means.

On the way to Mount Mitchell, I got lost and stopped to ask for directions in a town called Black Mountain, also known as "The Little Town that Rocks." The local townspeople encouraged me to return there after visiting Mount Mitchell. I made an effort to visit again on my way back down from the mountain, but unfortunately the town had shut down by the time I arrived. I was bummed. I could only window-shop, peeking through the glass of a few stores. However, I experienced great delight in taking pictures of, and sitting in, many colorful, beautifully hand-painted rocking chairs that were spread throughout the artsy town. It literally was a town that rocked!

A Vow to My Heart

Tuesday morning, before heading to the "She Speaks" conference, a houseguest named Mary surprised me during breakfast when she pulled out a gift for me, a poem titled "A Vow to My Heart," printed on beautiful artwork. I had only briefly met Mary when she arrived at the cottage Sunday evening. I came to find out that while I had been writing my poem atop Mount Mitchell, Mary simultaneously had been shopping for gifts and purchased the poem where I had window-shopped… in Black Mountain, The Little Town that Rocks! My heart was touched as I read the poem, an encouragement to stay true to my heart by living out my truth and owing no explanation to anyone. This thoughtful *heart gift of HOPE* continues to encourage me. In awe of God's goodness, I am reminded of His watchful eye over me, and His promise: "Every good and perfect gift is from above, coming down from the Father of heavenly lights…." (James 1:17 NIV)

A Heart with JOY and HOPE

In the hotel in Charlotte where the "She Speaks" conference was being held, a woman accidentally collided with me. We apologized to each other, then shook hands as we briefly exchanged our names. Her name was Annette. That was the extent of our conversation that day. But the very next morning, as my assigned roommate, Pamela, and I entered a huge conference room that was packed with over 700 attendees, and while the worship/praise song "10,000 Reasons" by Matt Redman was playing, Annette chased me down, grabbed my arm, and began to put a bracelet on me — one with a heart-shaped charm. Pamela and I were surprised and couldn't understand why Annette was putting the bracelet on my wrist. When I looked at the bracelet, the heart charm had my name, "JOY," on it. I looked up at Annette wondering why she, a woman I didn't even know except for her name, was giving me a bracelet with my name on it. She then explained, "Last night while praying, The Holy Spirit prompted me to give this to you." In awe I replied, "The Holy Spirit what? Told you to give this to me?" She nodded her head, saying, "Yes." I gave her a hug and thanked her. I looked at the bracelet again but the heart-shaped charm had flipped to other side, revealing the word "HOPE." My mouth dropped open. I then asked her if she knew the reason why I was attending the conference. She responded, "No."

Joyful Messenger of HOPE

But I knew. I had prayed for God to remove fear and doubt, and to confirm that I am called to be a joyful messenger of HOPE. On November 17th, 2012, eight months prior to the "She Speaks" conference, I had surrendered my whole heart to God saying, "I'll do anything you want me to do, go anywhere you want me to go, and say anything you want me to say. I'm yours. Just tell me." God's Spirit gently responded with a whisper upon my heart: "Go share my hope." Later that same day, God's Spirit, in a very unexpected way, downloaded into my heart, mind, and soul a specific message about this word spelled H-O-P-E which we all desperately need for a life of lasting joy: "**H**is **O**wn **P**ersonal **E**ncouragement™."

My journey has called me to persevere through much in my lifetime. Through childhood traumas to present-day traumas and many other painful and difficult circumstances in between, I've learned how to persevere, and through perseverance discovered the secrets to being joyful in HOPE. So it is an honor and privilege to be able to share an encouraging message in my forthcoming book, as I let readers in on my personal transformational journey that is happening because

23

of HOPE. It's my heart's desire that through my book, you and many others will be inspired to fully embrace HOPE and experience joy no matter what circumstances you face.

God's Gifts and Precious Promises

Some people call the *heart gifts of HOPE* I received *sweet serendipity,* meaning "good fortune" or "luck." But I believe the outpouring of blessings that include the promises of Scripture are encouragements from God to remind us all of His great love and plans for us. "For I know the plans I have for you," declares the LORD, "plans to prosper you and not to harm you, plans to give you hope and a future." (Jeremiah 29:11 NIV)

Finding Joy, HOPE, and Your Destiny

Can you recall a season when you experienced difficult circumstances that led you to your knees to cry out for Divine help? Or maybe you're in the midst of challenging circumstances that are overwhelming you with doubts about how to move forward towards your destiny with any kind of joy or hope? I understand. I have been in those shoes. I'm here to encourage you to have faith and keep seeking God with all your heart. "And without faith, it is impossible to please God, because anyone who comes to him must believe he exists and that he rewards those who earnestly seek him." (Hebrews 11:6 NIV)

My prayer blessing for you comes from the Scriptures: "May the God of hope fill you with all joy and peace as you trust in Him so that you may overflow with hope by the power of the Holy Spirit." (Romans 15:13 NIV)

"Bea" Joy Christianna B's mission is to BLESS and INSPIRE others wherever her heart takes her, radiating LIGHT and LOVE through soulful messages of HOPE with JOY. She rejoices in being an encourager through the spoken and written word, including her love for sharing poetry and other "heart gifts of HOPE." To find out more about the special "heart gift" she wants to share with you and the world visit: www.HOPEwithJOY.com

How to Care for a Masterpiece

Dr. Reggie Blount, Ph.D.

"I saw the angel in the marble and carved until I set him free."
~ Michelangelo

THERE IS A VERSE IN THE BIBLE that caught my attention many years ago that literally changed my life. The verse begins with "We are God's Masterpiece." (Ephesians 2:10, New Living Translation)

We are God's Masterpiece!

These words took me by surprise when I first read them. *Could it be that we,* could it be that I was a masterpiece made by God?

A masterpiece...
A one of a kind original...
A priceless work of art...

Could it be that every human being, including myself, was created by God to be God's greatest piece of work, a masterpiece?

The discovery of these words began a journey of real transformation in my life. My faith taught me that God created me and that I was loved by God, so I never doubted God's love for me because I experienced it over and over again. Growing up poor in a single-parent household in an urban community made for a challenging upbringing. Much of my experience was immersed in an environment of "not enough" — not enough money and sometimes not enough food or other basic needs. Yet I experienced more than enough love, especially through the members of a neighborhood church that had an amazing children and youth ministry. It was through them I learned that God loved me, because of how the people of that congregation loved me and the other children in the community. I never doubted that God loved me.

But as much as I knew God's love for me, it never occurred to me that God created me to be His masterpiece. It never occurred to me that I was a priceless work of art in God's eyes. Part of the trauma of my upbringing was continually questioning my worth and value. There were many voices that had me believing that I might be loved, but my life really had no value. I found myself struggling much in my early life with issues of self-esteem and self-worth. You see, when you grow up in an environment of "not enough" you find yourself wrestling with questions like "Am I enough? Does my life have meaning? Does my life have purpose? When it is all said and done, will my life really matter? Will my life make a difference?"

One of my biggest life lessons is that what you think determines how you feel which determines how you act. When you've been shaped by a not-enough environment and find yourself feeling and asking over and over again, "Am I enough?" you begin to make choices that reinforce a life of not enough. Those choices sabotaged my efforts and ensured that I lived a life of not enough — because I believed I was not enough. I experienced many successes in my life, even becoming the first in my family to earn a Ph.D. Yet with all of my successes, I found it difficult to shake the imposter syndrome — that of feeling like a fraud and not being worthy of the successes I had achieved. When thoughts of "not enough" cause you to feel like an impostor, you make life choices to validate that you really are an impostor.

But life began to change when I discovered these words:

We are God's Masterpiece!

That phrase caused me to ask myself, "What would my life be like if I truly believed that I was God's masterpiece? What if I truly believed that I was created to live the masterpiece life God created for me?" I began to realize that if I truly was God's masterpiece called to live a masterpiece life, then I must address whatever was hindering me from living the life I was created to live. I understood that if I was to live that life, then, like Michelangelo, I must see the angel (the masterpiece) in me, hew away the rough walls that imprisoned me, and set the masterpiece free!

It was during this time of revelations that I was also doing my doctoral research on the faith formation of adolescents. In doing this research I identified "seven spiritual yearnings" I believe young people wrestle with in their spiritual development. They are identity, purpose, intimacy, healing, mentoring, nurture, and courage.

- Identity: A yearning to understand who they are; to answer the question "Who am I?" or "Whose am I?" A yearning to understand what it means to be made in the image of God, as in "Who am I in God's greater story?"

- Purpose: A yearning to understand their reason for being; to be able to answer "Why am I here? What role do I play in God's greater story?"

- Intimacy: A yearning to be loved unconditionally by God, family, and society.

- Healing: A yearning to be made whole again after experiencing various levels of brokenness.

- Mentoring: A yearning for a caring and wise guide who is interested enough to help them navigate the waters between adolescence and adulthood.

- Nurture: A yearning to be encouraged and empowered in the midst of their faith journey.

- Courage: A yearning for the strength to live boldly, fearlessly, and faithfully.

As I shared these yearnings in my classes and workshops, it was amazing to discover that these desires are not strictly confined to adolescents. I vividly remember a class session in which I presented these spiritual longings of young people and a thirty-year-old student began to cry because she realized these were yearnings she still longed to have satisfied in her life.

I have now come to realize that at any stage of your life you can find yourself experiencing a crisis of meaning that creates these yearnings for identity, purpose, intimacy, healing, mentoring, nurture, and courage. I now believe that these can be satisfied and your crisis of meaning healed when you allow yourself to believe that you are a masterpiece. Your work is to "carve" away those things that are holding you back from living the masterpiece life you were created to live. Your work is to set yourself, the masterpiece, free!

So how do you care for a masterpiece?

If you are to live the masterpiece life you were created to live, you must see the angel (the masterpiece) inside yourself, hew away the rough walls that imprison your uniqueness, and set the masterpiece free! It's carving away all thoughts of not enough that allows you to discover that as God's masterpiece you are more than enough. God has given you more than enough ability to climb, to shine, and to soar!

I believe you can best care for the masterpiece if you care for yourself by not only breaking free of limiting beliefs, but also choosing to live free. You can best do this by satisfying the seven spiritual yearnings for identity, purpose, intimacy, healing, mentoring, nurture, and courage.

Be Free to Claim Your Name (Identity)

It is a natural desire for all of us to know who we are. "Who am I?" is one of the most pivotal questions of life. But as a masterpiece, "Who am I?" should not be the question you ask because it is not helpful, enriching, edifying, or life-giving. It leaves the task of discovery resting solely on your shoulders and puts the onus on you to fill in the blanks. I believe that this question needs rephrasing to ask instead, *"Whose am I?"* This allows you to discover the real longing, the real yearning you have, and that is to answer, "To whom do I belong?" The answer? You are God's masterpiece! Your true identity is lost when you define yourself by what your not-enough self thinks you are, or by what you allow others to say you are, rather than by who you really are: God's masterpiece!

Be Free to Live Purposefully

I believe you are a masterpiece not just in form, but also in function. You were created to live purposefully. Your life has purpose and meaning. No one is here by accident, and there is a divine assignment for us all. Some call it a vocation; others name it a calling. Author Frederick Buechner, in his book *Wishful Thinking: A Theological ABC,* says, "The place God calls you to is the place where your deep gladness and the world's deep hunger meet." It's at that intersection of your passion and the world's need that you discover purpose.

31

Be Free to Receive Healing

My research has shown me that by the time they reach their teenage years almost all young people have experienced some type of brokenness, rejection, ridicule, emotional or physical pain, shame, guilt, oppression, or demoralization. When the brokenness goes unaddressed and has never had the opportunity to heal, it is carried into adulthood where it ends up affecting the life choices they make. Caring for the masterpiece within you includes acknowledging your brokenness and being free and vulnerable enough to receive the restoration you need to live the masterpiece life you were created to live.

Be Free to Love (Intimacy)

In her book *The Gift of Imperfection,* Brené Brown says, "A deep sense of love and belonging is an irreducible need of all people. We are biologically, cognitively, physically, and spiritually wired to love, to be loved, and to belong." She goes on to say, "We cultivate love when we allow our most vulnerable and powerful selves to be deeply seen and known, and we honor the spiritual connection that grows from that offering with trust, respect, kindness and affection." It is a natural, spiritual desire to long to belong to someone who loves you. When you know you belong to someone who loves you, you have no problem embracing and possessing that relationship as your own. To believe you are God's masterpiece is to believe you are deeply seen and known by God, which then allows you to be free to be deeply seen and known by others.

Be Free to Be Mentored

We all yearn for a guide, especially if we are navigating paths we've never experienced. You need mentors who are open enough to testify concerning their struggles and challenges and offer you the tools and pathways to free the masterpiece within. You need mentors or role models who are willing to share their journey with you and offer insight, guidance, hope, and some direction to help you thrive in living the masterpiece life you were created to live.

Be Free to Be Nurtured

As I said earlier, you are God's masterpiece not just in form but also in function. To maximize your masterpiece life means to strive to grow and develop daily. To be nurtured is to be willing to allow others to offer you the care and attention you need to continue to grow and develop.

Be Free to Live Fearlessly (Courage)

Theodore Roosevelt is quoted as saying:

> It is not the critic who counts; not the man who points out how the strong man stumbles, or where the doer of deeds could have done them better. The credit belongs to the man who is actually in the arena, whose face is marred by dust and sweat and blood; who strives valiantly; who errs, who comes short again and again, because there is no effort without error and shortcoming; but who does actually strive to do the deeds... who spends himself in a worthy cause; who at the best knows in the end the triumph of high achievement, and who at the worst, if he fails, at least fails while daring greatly.

If you are to truly live the masterpiece life you were created to live then you must free yourself to get into the arena of life – to take risks, strive, stumble, sweat, and dare greatly. Living fearlessly isn't living without fear; it's living boldly in spite of the fears.

33

My life is transformed daily by knowing and truly believing I am God's masterpiece! We are all God's masterpieces called to live out the divine assignments, the divine purposes our lives were created to be. And as we strive to satisfy our spiritual yearnings, we become able to more clearly see the masterpiece lives designed for us.

Let's go forth and truly live the lives we were created to embrace!

Dr. Reggie Blount, Ph.D. "The Masterpiece Living Coach," has over twenty years of experience as a pastor, professor, and agent of hope and transformation. As a transformational leader he is committed to aiding people in discovering their divine purpose and living the masterpiece life they were created to live. Learn more about *How to Care for a Masterpiece* at www.CaringForAMasterpiece.com.

Finishing the Dance

Yolanda Bradford

WHEN I WAS ABOUT TWELVE, my mother married a man who was enlisted in the military. I soon learned that not only was I going to have a stepfather, but our family would be moving to the island of Oahu in Hawaii. I didn't know much about Hawaii, only what I had learned in school and what I had occasionally viewed on television shows and movies that were filmed there. Nevertheless I was overcome with excitement about escaping my humdrum life in Oklahoma City. To me, my stepfather was my savior because I had privately dreamed of leaving the red dirt of Oklahoma, where my life was filled with anguish and unhappiness, and moving to a different state where I could reinvent myself. To me he represented the doorway to a new life, so I was very hopeful when I learned that we were moving to Hawaii. I truly believed I would find my voice, learn to speak up for myself, and step out of the shadows of my fears.

Our new home was located in Schofield Barracks, a military base that was located on the northwest side of the island. It was surrounded by the lush greenery of the mountains and rows upon rows of palm trees and flowers with fragrant scents that were new to my senses. Yes, the view of my life had changed so drastically that I often pinched myself to make sure that I was not dreaming.

I was excited about attending school in Hawaii because I hoped to be free of being bullied and called "stuck up" simply because my peers misunderstood that it was my shyness that crippled my interactions with them and that it was not a choice I purposely made. I believed that I would no longer be judged by my outward appearance, my hair, or my ethnicity. I truly longed to be free of all judgements and just wanted to be accepted as me.

Unlike some other military bases where the schools are located on the premises, Schofield Barracks was different. All military children had to attend local schools. I was in awe with the thought that I would be able to meet real Hawaiians.

I was soon enrolled in Wahiawa Heights Middle School. It was the most beautiful campus I had ever seen. The buildings were painted orange with a bright yellow trim. There were no closed corridors or hallways, and all the doors accessed the manicured grounds surrounding the school. The school consisted of three main concrete buildings, and at the end of each were the boys' and girls' bathrooms. Each bathroom area was dedicated to specific groups and I quickly learned the location of the "military brats" bathrooms. I didn't agree with this antiquated system of separation because it might limit me in making friends with a real Hawaiian. Although I was happy with my new friends who came from various states, I was disappointed that our conversations were limited to stories from our home states. Although some of them were humorous and exciting, I longed to learn the stories of the people of Hawaii.

As ideas danced around in my mind about how to create camaraderie between the different social groups, one day I mustered up enough courage to speak up and introduce my idea about how we should all intermingle. Unfortunately my suggestion was quickly shot down by the teacher, and so were my courage and ideas. I quietly took my place in the shadows of the imaginary barriers that existed between the groups.

When picking my class electives, I chose to learn how to play the ukulele and signed up to learn traditional Hawaiian dance. I noticed on my enrollment form that physical education and a cooking class were on my schedule and I desired to take neither of them. I begged the counselor to allow me to drop the cooking class, and especially the physical education class because I was not very athletic and was at an awkward age at which I was physically developing at a rapid pace. I did not feel comfortable in my skin. But as fate would have it, both courses were on the required class list.

The girls' locker room was a stark contrast from the colorful classroom buildings that were in keeping with the beautiful flower beds. Painted a gloomy grey with off-white accents, it gave the impression of being a prison. In the center of the room above everyone was the warden's watchtower. To the right of her tower were the lockers and benches where the open showers were located. Directly in front of the tower were private showers covered by a thin, off-white shower curtain, which could only be used by girls who were on their menstrual cycle. Everyone was required to shower after gym class in the open-air showers unless you were on your period. The ritual required that each girl was to undress and towel up where the lockers were located, then everyone had to stop by the warden's watchtower and open her towel to demonstrate that she was prepared to shower.

One day I entered the locker room with caution after gym class was over and located a secluded space in the corner where I began to slowly undress, timing my movements so that by the time I was ready the other girls would be just about finished taking their showers. As I walked toward the warden's judgment tower, barefoot and shivering from walking on cold concrete, I stood there frozen, unable to succumb to the ritual of opening my towel. I was abruptly woken from my stupor when I heard the warden bellowing out for me to open my towel. Looking downward I shamefully lied and told the warden that I was on my cycle. I was then given permission to enter the sanctuary of one of the private showers.

37

I continued this sham for two weeks. The rhythmic dance of the struggle between my personal privacy and the ancient procedure of the school's policies came to a screeching halt the day the warden asked me to either remove my towel or present a note from my doctor explaining my prolonged menstrual cycle. I defiantly refused to participate in the waltz of exposing the outer essence of myself and failed the class because of the shame I held about the awkwardness of my body.

By the time my junior year in high school rolled around, my family had been relocated to Fort Campbell, Kentucky, where I attended Fort Campbell High School. By this time I had escaped deep into my shell and had no desire to make new friends or participate in any activities.

Again, one of the required courses was physical education, a course that I deeply hated. I had no choice but to take it because a failure would lower my GPA and change some of my college choices. As I entered the gymnasium, I first glanced at the wooden bleachers against the wall that could extend and retract. Looking over to my right I viewed the climbing rope as it hung down from the ceiling. I also noticed the black scuff marks on the walls that indicated where balls had hit them. I wondered how many students had been hurt or harmed playing the game of dodge ball. Looking around at all the other apparatus in the gymnasium only brought me painful memories of my failure at Wahiawa Heights.

In my orientation class with my gym teacher, I was given the curriculum and her expectation of me in the class. Secretly I believed she had been in contact with the warden from my former school. I was informed that I would be required to participate in the annual dance recital, which would be performed in front of the entire student body. Most of the other girls were already grouped together. Unfortunately, as I was a new transfer and didn't belong to a group, my gym teacher finally noticed a cluster of girls that did not have the minimum number of people, and I ended up with other girls who were equally as shy as I was.

Our assignment was to choreograph a five-to-ten-minute dance routine, which required us to use a prescribed amount of floor space and to either start from the floor and end up standing, or vice versa. In our initial rehearsals, I'm sure our movements resembled fish flopping around looking for life-sustaining water! We were clumsy in our movements, our timing was completely off, and we lacked rhythm and balance. We collectively decided to increase our practice time because we knew we were the joke of the class and all of our peers were just waiting for us to fail.

The extra hours and days of training began to pay off, and we began to move as one unit. The synchronicity of our timing improved greatly and soon we started to move with the grace of ballerinas. The struggle of balance and rhythmic movements that existed in the beginning soon disappeared and we were one in the natural flow of our dance. My confidence soared because the extra hours we had dedicated to our dance had paid off. We were in sync and I was comfortable with my new friends. I truly believed that I would triumphantly complete the school recital.

On the day of the recital, as I looked out into the audience at the student body and at our group, my knees begin to shake and my hands became hot and sweaty. I could feel my stomach start to boil like hot lava that spills out from an active volcano. I then took another look at my classmates and thought of the camaraderie that had been created between us during rehearsals. I thought to myself that if I couldn't do this for myself, then I could certainly do it for them. I so desperately did not want to let them down, so I took a deep breath and kept my mind on the task at hand. However, as we inched closer and closer to the stage, I began to fall farther and farther behind my group.

When the hour came for my group to perform, I was standing at the back of the stage. As I caught a glimpse of their eyes searching for me, I began to weep. I had lost all confidence in my ability to perform because the fear of facing my peers had stifled me. I had let down my newfound friends, but more important, I had let myself down again. I had chosen to not allow my light to shine. I didn't stand up for myself and I had given in to a belief that I did not quite understand at that time, namely that my place was in the shadows of others. I surrendered to my fears and failed to complete the dance.

I took solace in a corner of the gym and curled up in the fetal position. As I sat there awash in a pool of self-pity and shame and what seemed to be one of the lowest points in my life, a small, frail voice from deep within me began to speak hope into my existence. I knew what I must begin to do in my life to change things, so at that moment I made the decision to use my voice and place myself in situations in which I had opportunities to speak up and be seen. I decided that I would step out of the shadow of others and my fears. I would finish my next dance in life... no matter what!

Moving forward, the flow of my life changed. I joined the band and became part of the color guard as a flag bearer, and won best-dressed female my senior year. My first job was with a fast food chain, where initially I worked in the background of the restaurant cooking and cleaning. One day a position became available working the front counter taking orders and speaking with customers. I jumped at the opportunity to move from the shadows into the light of day. As my first customer approached, I smiled from deep within because I was in the flow of the dance of releasing my voice.

Looking back on my memories of being a young, frightened girl who struggled to find her voice and be seen, I now realize the courage and inner strength we all must call upon to allow our light to shine in this world. If we are to become the beacons of hope that we are meant to be, and let our voices be heard, we must persevere, no matter how daunting the "dance" might be.

Yolanda Bradford is a transformational speaker and leader who teaches people how to liberate themselves from wounds of the past and step into their full authentic expression in the world. Her BA in metaphysics combined with her powerful presence as a teacher is what draws people to her for their own healing and transformation. You can learn more about Yolanda's services and her forthcoming book, *My Mother's Womb,* at www.YolandaBradford.com.

Not What I Expected

Andria Corso

IN DECEMBER OF 2013 I WAS FLYING HOME from my final business trip of the year, exhausted and in dire need of a break. Thankful that the holidays were approaching and I could take time off, I decided I needed and wanted to start having more fun in my life. *"What if I made 2014 my year of fun?"* I thought. *"What if everything I chose to do in the coming year was in some way, either directly or indirectly, related to having more fun? What would that be like?"* I felt myself light up inside. *"It would be, like, FUN!"* I set the intention on my flight home: 2014 would be my year of fun. I couldn't wait to see what adventures and experiences awaited me with that simple decision to have fun as the foundation of the next year. Little did I know what was in store for me that coming year...

Fast-forward to April, 2014, when I found myself in a hospital in a surgeon's consultation room getting news that my vibrant, fit, always healthy and health-conscious dad had stage three pancreatic cancer. Sucker punch in the gut. *"What the heck? How could this be?"* I was in shock. It felt surreal, as if I'd stepped into a bad dream or someone else's life.

My dad and I had a close, yet complicated relationship. When I was twelve, he left our family for another woman and I became filled with anger and resentment. It was a vulnerable age when "Daddy's approval" meant everything to me, yet he wasn't there to provide that to me. My emotional development was arrested. I spent my life from that point forward living a dysfunctional pattern of constantly seeking his approval. I made all my decisions, subconsciously, based on what I knew he would want and what he would do. I lived my life based on his operating principles. He was my anchor and my foundation.

Now suddenly he was sick. And even more suddenly, he was gone — five months from diagnosis to his death, which was unfathomable to me. I barely had time to process the fact that he had pancreatic cancer and then he was dead. The very foundation of how I lived my life cracked with his diagnosis and fully collapsed when he passed away. I was falling, rudderless, into a deep pit of sorrow. I had no idea how to live without him as my anchor. This was not exactly the year of fun I expected.

In the midst of all of this, one of my dogs was diagnosed with malignant GI lymphoma, the worst possible cancer a dog can get. There I was, in the middle of what was supposed to be my year of fun, and my dad gets diagnosed with the worst possible cancer a human can get (not that any of them are good, but pancreatic cancer is in a league of its own with five-year survival rates less than six percent), then my dog gets diagnosed with the worst possible cancer a dog can get. They passed away exactly two weeks apart. My heart broke into a million pieces. I was brought to my knees with grief.

Year of fun? Hardly. Yet little did I know this was actually a divinely orchestrated perfect storm; a series of events that propelled me onto a journey of spiritual growth and awakening unlike anything I'd ever experienced; one that caused me to not only shed my identity (that was so closely aligned with my dad, his approval, and his value system), but also to reestablish my foundation and re-create my identity as one that is now grounded in the certainty of aligning with divine will. Yes, me, a fiercely left-brained person who lived from the ego-mind, now chooses to live from the place of surrendering to the Divine.

Do not be mistaken; this was not an easy journey. However, it is one that I am eternally grateful for and that has drastically transformed my life for the better.

After my dad passed away, I realized my entire existence was based on his life philosophy and my need for his approval. Most of this stems from my parents' divorce and my dad leaving our family when I was at such a vulnerable age. Although we maintained a decent relationship, we didn't grow close until I was in my twenties. By then my habitual behaviors of acting subconsciously for his approval had taken root. After he passed, I also recognized how much of my life and decision-making had been based on false fears — fear of failure, loss, rejection, disapproval, losing control, etc. Many of these fears were formed during the trauma from my parents' divorce. However, it wasn't until my dad passed away that I became aware of these things. My identity and how I lived my life was completely wrapped up in him. When he died, that foundation fell away. Even though I'd known for many years at a soul level that I was not living my life authentically, I never changed anything. Despite many attempts to free myself from the need for "Daddy's approval," I wasn't able to fully make the break.

When he died, the break was made. It was somewhat of a relief and also filled with feelings of guilt and grief. I was finally free, and yet I didn't want to feel the pain of losing him. I felt guilty feeling freed by his passing; I felt deep sadness that he was gone. I was uncertain of what my life would even look like without having the constant thought in the back of my head: "What will Daddy think?" My dad was always very supportive of every decision I made and at the same time his influence on my life was overwhelming. I chose my career and my business because of his influence. I tried repeatedly to change my career focus, but always reverted back to what he advised and thought was best. And yes, I did this until I was forty-four years old and he died. I'm almost embarrassed to write that sentence. How many forty-year-olds are wandering around thinking about what their dad will say each time they make a major life decision? And yet, that was me. Then he was gone and it all changed. I embraced the fact that I no longer wanted to live my life based on the fearful decision-making practices I had learned and mastered over the past thirty years. I wanted to let go of my ego-driven fear-based model and start living life from a place of faith, freedom, and flow. I had no idea how to even do this or if it were even possible for me, but I was going to find out.

His passing pushed me to let go of what my mind thought to be true and feel into what my heart knew to be true. I embarked on a year-long journey to not only heal from the loss of my dad and the agony of watching pancreatic cancer take his life from the inside out, but also to heal from the anger and sadness of thirty-year-old wounds that I had carried with me since my parents' divorce. I also had to heal and grieve the loss of my sweet dog. As the title of Elizabeth Lesser's book says, I was *Broken Open*. I opened up to what is truly possible when we let go of identifying with our ego and fear-based mindset and what is truly possible when we step into our soul and live life from a "Divine Self" perspective. My year of fun turned into a year of loss, but that is not the theme of this story or where it ends.

As 2014 progressed, my life shifted repeatedly with each phone call from and doctor's report about my dad. With each event I gained more and more perspective about life and somehow gained more and more strength to deal with the cards we were handed. Each time I thought it couldn't get worse, it did. Each time I'd think he couldn't possibly be any thinner or look any worse than when I last saw him, he would. And each time I could not bear to think of what he must be going through, someone was there to pick me up. I found comfort in places and from people I didn't know existed the prior year. The perfectly timed phone calls, texts, emails, and cards of comfort from so many of my friends and extended family members always arrived exactly when I needed them. There were blessings and gifts everywhere. Despite the fact that my dad was suffering, there were blessings all around us.

46

Somehow, when I was sure I would not be able to get through another day at his bedside, I found strength deep inside me. I was lifted by my own faith and belief that there is a greater plan for us all. Even if we don't understand it, we must believe it is meant for our good. This was the plan for my dad.

Have I accepted it? Not yet. I imagine that will come in time. Yet my faith is strong and I know he is in a better place.

The year was also about being present. Knowing my time with my dad was finite made each moment with him one to cherish. I imagine life would be much better if we acknowledged that this is true for all of us — not just those who are terminally ill. Imagine how we'd treat each other if we knew that each moment could be our last and our time was running out. I took full advantage of knowing this about my dad. I told him everything I ever wanted to say. I repeated things I knew he knew about how much I adored him, how much he had taught me, how his voice would be in my head forever, and his love and strength in my heart always. I said it all and then some. I remember thinking that he must be sick of hearing me tell him how much I love him, and then I knew that was impossible.

My year of fun turned into my year of loss which turned into my year of gifts. I received the gift of strength from others and from God. I received the gift of knowing my time with my dad was fleeting, and the gift of recognizing what is truly important in life. I was also given the gift of perspective which, looking back, is what I needed more than anything and certainly what I needed more than fun. Without the perspective about life that I gained during that year, I'm not sure I would have fully experienced the joy of living a year of fun. I also don't know if I would have been present enough to fully enjoy it. It's amazing that we always get exactly what we need even when we don't know we need it.

A year of terrible loss also opened me up for the journey of a lifetime — one of spiritual growth and awakening. In addition to the blessings that showed up during the suffering was my heart breaking open to the true transformational journey that occurred in the year following all the loss; one that led me from living a life based on fear to living in the flow of the authentic rhythm of my Divine Self.

I had set an intention to have a year of fun and what I got was not at all what I expected, but so much more. Despite what the year felt and looked like as it occurred, there was a divine plan at work — one that propelled me to transform my life in amazing ways. As I look back, it is all so clear: regardless of what we see in front of us, we must have faith and believe that everything is always working out for the best. It may not be what we expect, but is always according to a divine plan that is ultimately meant for our good.

Andria Corso is an award-winning executive leadership, career, and life coach, an author, and the founder of AndriaCorso & Co. Her latest book, *Fear to Flow: How to Let Go of Your Struggle and Allow Life to Unfold Perfectly,* will be published in June, 2016. To learn more and to receive a free audio on *How to Overcome the Top Five Fears that Keep You Stuck and Struggling,* please visit www.AndriaCorso.com.

~೨~

TIYALO Mahalo!
Practice Thanks for Resilience, Good Fortune, and Success

Joseph Grace

LIFE BRINGS THE WORST… and the best to us. Our job is to make the best of what comes our way without withdrawing and becoming islands. We can do that by making the best of ourselves, the best for our loved ones, and making and keeping ourselves prepared for what life brings.

Take TIYALO Mahalo! to heart, and be thankful for life's gifts and your good fortune.

"TIYALO Mahalo!" is the combination of an acronym, "TIYALO" – Trust In Yourself And Loved Ones, and the Hawaiian phrase *mahalo*, which translated to English means "Thank you!" I've combined these two phrases to mean "Give thanks for your life, gifts, and good fortune!" as a reminder to express gratitude as a big part of my life.

And here's the biggest little secret of TIYALO Mahalo!: **Be thankful in as many ways as you can!**

With that preview, let's look closer at the challenges and opportunities of TIYALO Mahalo!

Adversity in the Free World

Too often in the modern world, freedom is an illusion and choice is a mirage. The choices we make are often made for us, the justice we seek is not available, the promises on which we rely turn out to be subterfuge, or the service or product for which we pay is a sham. When we are taken advantage of or realize our "free world" is not so free after all, we can get frustrated. During these reality checks and paradigm shifts, all too often we lose perspective.

I get very frustrated trying to fix situations that are clearly illicit, predatory, and/or pernicious, but which resist correction. And I get even more frustrated when I find these issues are all but unfixable and that the "authorities" are less a part of the solution and more a shameless part of the problem. For example, local professionals; legal counsel; industry watchdogs; local police; FBI; "independent" experts; the local court system, judges, and court officers; or generally any local bully or gangster — all of these authorities sometimes fail. In other words, I get very frustrated at holes in our "democracy" where special interests have taken control of a slice or chunk of our commons, government, lives, finances, rights, liberties, happiness, or freedom. The cascading frustration is long term and corrosive, especially when it persists and cuts too close to home or daily life for comfort.

So when I came upon a simple coping strategy for my frustration and consequent doldrums, I decided to share it because I believe we are all subject to these predatory forms of theft, harassment, and passive aggression in the modern free world. We could all use some rest and relief as we cope with adversity or, with determination, rise to fight the good fight.

The core strength of TIYALO Mahalo! is you. The first line of defense is always you.

Trust in Yourself and Loved Ones (TIYALO)

Trust in yourself requires having strength in yourself. And if you can trust yourself, you can be there for those whom you support and who support you.

Loved ones are all those who care for us, and those for whom we care – anyone who drives us to be the best we can be. They are also those who depend on us and on whom we depend. Parents, family, and children can be great sources of strength in our drive to overcome obstacles and even dire circumstances. But our support network can include extended family and close friends.

Ultimately we have to be strong internally most of all, even if we derive strength from others sometimes. And one of the best ways to be strong is to know ourselves and give thanks for all our gifts and good fortune.

Mahalo! (Hawaiian: Thank You!)

We come into the world dependent on others, but we mature into adults and good citizens by growing as individuals. Along the way we take so many things for granted: health, family, education, home, monies, society, and opportunity.

In emergencies or times of reflection, we can renew our spirits by giving thanks for our gifts and good fortune. By gifts I mean, first of all, our inner aptitudes, strengths, and skills, and second, our closest mentors and supporters. They belong to our core, and no one and nothing can take them away. They help define us. When we recall our gifts, we recall our strengths and our allies.

And we give thanks for our good fortune, the blessings we may take for granted but that bless us with the opportunities of modern life: everything from eyeglasses (or lasik surgery), telephones, books, libraries, and gyms, to peace. Society abounds with valuable information and overwhelming opportunity. Sometimes we need to slow down, remember how lucky we are (even in adverse circumstances), and transcend our situation until we center ourselves.

TIYALO Mahalo!: Center Yourself with Trust and Thanks

Recalling our trust in ourselves and in those we love, and giving thanks for all our good fortune, gives us breathing room and perspective to distance ourselves from nasty situations. I find that TIYALO Mahalo! gives me a welcome dose of perspective when I feel trapped or threatened. If I can recall how lucky I am, even despite the current predatory (and perhaps fruitless or frustrating) situation, I often find my composure. I can center myself, regain composure, deal with the situation(s) better, and cope with a renewed sense of self, spirit, and perspective. Perhaps I can better assess my situation and options, too. Gaining center can be key to coping.

Thanks: The Path to Inner Strength, Good Luck, and Success

Even better than coping is preparing for whatever may come our way. We need life habits and strategies to prepare ourselves so we can avoid danger and risk in the future. Giving thanks is the key. Being thankful gives us not only reflection, but many paths for preparing and taking action.

The first and obvious way to give thanks is through self-reflection and taking inventory of our gifts, strengths, friends, and family. TIYALO refers us to our loved ones and those we love dearly. Both are valuable drivers for our lives. We will still have resources and gifts (even if they are just the roof over our heads, electricity, and hot water — or even just running water) that we take for granted. Self-reflection about ourselves, our strengths, friends, family, and loved ones helps us understand ourselves and appreciate our abilities, support, challenges, and opportunities.

Another crucial way to give thanks for your gifts and good fortune is simply to use them. Be thankful for your gifts and good fortune and practice thanks by using them and honing them. Practice, practice, practice. When you use them with care and thanks, you build your strengths, good habits, and good fortune.

"Diligence is the mother of good luck."
~ *Benjamin Franklin*

Without preparation, life is full of challenge. With preparation, life offers a wealth of opportunity. Preparation gives us choice, and with good decisions we make our own good luck.

Live a Thankful, Bountiful Life

Be thankful for all you have – your circumstances, challenges, and opportunities – and do that by leading your life with **appreciation and preparation**. Be thankful for your strengths by leading your life prepared, growing your strengths, and making your own opportunities of new challenges and situations. Use your thanks to be yourself, know yourself, hone yourself, and prepare for what's to come. Live a thankful, bountiful life.

Seven Paths to Practice Thanks, Appreciation, and Preparation

We benefit by giving thanks for our own gifts, but our gifts are very diverse and occur in unique combinations (physical, mental, emotional, artistic, spiritual, etc.). So we need a way to practice them that works for all of us.

Show appreciation by tending your special aptitudes and abilities by touching *bases of gratitude*. Challenge yourself with new obligations and opportunities. You have a surprising number of choices and different paths to follow, but I list seven bases of gratitude below that any of us can practice.

The Seven Bases of Gratitude

Please practice the core ones whenever possible and touch on the latter ones as they resonate with you or offer you the opportunity to practice. Practice will strengthen you, make you more exceptional, and support those you love.

The Core Four

1. **Thanks** – Strengthen your spirit; fortitude: Appreciate gifts, good fortune, life, opportunity, and happiness. TIYALO Mahalo!

2. **Reflection** – Strengthen your integrity; intuition: Know yourself. For inspiration read *The Seven Habits of Highly Effective People* by Steven Covey.

3. **Perspective** – Strengthen your perception; clarity: Less is (often) more. For inspiration read *The Power of Less* by Leo Babauta.

4. **Self-Expression** – Strengthen your voice; motivation: Aspire. For inspiration read *Drive: The Surprising Truth About What Motivates Us* by Daniel Pink.

The Bold Three

1. **Support** – Help others by sharing and caring: Share the good (and bad) with family, friends, supporters, and loved ones. Practice good family values.

2. **Care** – Help others by listening and caring: Care for self and loved ones, and do good for others. Practice Good Samaritan values.

3. **Generosity** – Help others by giving and caring: Pay forward and build community, commons, and legacy. Practice good stewardship values.

These seven practices build gratitude and strength throughout your life. Practice them for strength in yourself and those close to you, and to contribute to the greater good. Be thankful and grateful for all that is good (and even not so great) in your life, and practice to be the best you can be.

New Beginning

TIYALO Mahalo! is just a beginning. It is perhaps the simplest and most basic suggestion you will ever receive, and yet perhaps the most powerful healthy habit.

It's risk-free. Without even alluding to wealth or prosperity, TIYALO reminds us to look to strength (ourselves, family, and friends), take stock of the immense wealth and opportunity of life, and maintain a generous, prosperous attitude – especially in adverse conditions.

And the hidden quality of TIYALO Mahalo! is that Mahalo! strengthens social fabric both inwardly and outwardly: a healthy dose of Mahalo! generates an unexpected boost in spirit from our natural internal feedback loop, and the external world often rewards those who strengthen community (á la Pay It Forward). The benefits may hide, but they do accumulate.

In other words, helping others is paradoxically a strengthening action for yourself. When at your weakest, most suppressed state, if you can find a way to help others you are also finding a way to regenerate your own spirit. And that is the key hidden strength and beauty of TIYALO Mahalo!

Most of all, remember to **be thankful in as many ways as you can!**

* For your reference, please find my Cheat Sheet: TIYALO Mahalo! on the next page.

Cheat Sheet: TIYALO Mahalo!

TIYALO – Trust In Yourself and Loved Ones: Family and friends are important. Look to yourself... and them for strength, support, and motivation.

Mahalo! – Give thanks, share, and support others: Everyone is important, and your heart is important. Look to be generous in pocket, mind, and most importantly heart. You not only strengthen your community, but you will often be surprised at your renewed spirit from within.

Seven Paths of TIYALO Mahalo! Practice

The Core Four

1. Thanks (spirit, fortitude): Appreciate life, opportunity, and happiness.

2. Reflection (integrity, intuition): Know yourself.

3. Perspective (perception, clarity): Simplify to clarify.

4. Self-Expression (voice, motivation): Aspire.

The Bold Three

1. Support (sharing, shouldering): Share the good (and bad). Practice good family values for family, friends, loved ones, and supporters.

2. Care (helping, listening): Do good for others. Practice Good Samaritan values.

3. Generosity (giving, maintaining): Pay forward, and build community, commons, and legacy. Practice good stewardship values.

Be thankful in as many ways as you can!

Joseph Grace is a software engineer by trade and had been lucky in life until about a decade ago. Since then he has persisted in turning some proverbial lemon investments into lemonade, but the unyielding and all-too-successful fraudsters resist! He has developed a powerful coping mechanism that he uses to deal with unyielding adversity. He shares his shift in thinking in the hope that his own life transformation will translate to resilience, good fortune, and success in yours.

www.CommonsCare™.com

Mastering Life-Path Flow

D. Marie Hanson, Ph.D.

MY LIFE-PATH AS A SEEKER OF AGE-OLD QUESTIONS… *What are we? Where did we come from? Where are we going?*… began at ten years old. I experienced a near-death experience (NDE). It was not like the ones I read about later; I did not "go far." Just far enough to launch my quest for meaning of my experience of an existence beyond the physical plane. My mind's focus was forever-after set on understanding the meaning of life as I lived it, as contrasted to the drowning I experienced in a wooded lake on a warm summer day.

As my consciousness was released from the pain and struggle to reach the air above me, my lungs pulled in cool water that soothed the acute burning sensation. My child-mind thought, *"No one told me you can breathe water!"* but the innocence of a child's mind was altered a moment later as I watched my body drift down to the lake bottom. I was not attached to that slender form in a bright red bathing suit. I stretched out into boundless space and sighed deeply. Like a foot released from walking in a tight shoe, I was so relieved to expand, to leave the cramped squeeze of my bodily form behind.

I can still remember the feel of the sharp stones cutting into my skin as the lifeguard pressed down on my bony chest to bring up the sour water squirting through my nose and mouth. I did not want to be back in that sore, exhausted body, nor did I speak of the experience I

59

had between drowning and being resuscitated on the shore. The drama that played out while I was drifting in a state I can only describe as bliss was mysterious and disturbing to my parents. Mother's experience of standing knee-deep in water screaming as she watched me go down was excruciating. She could not swim. My father's repeated futile attempts to find my body on the lake bottom shamed him. He was a powerful swimmer.

Synchronistic Miracle

The mystery of the man who saved my life took all our attention. As my mother stood on the shore screaming for help, an unknown man hurried forward. He was dropping his trousers as he called out, "I saw where she went down!" He dove in, and as my mother told it, he swam straight to where I was, submerged, and pulled me up, just as the lifeguard reached him to assist taking me to shore.

After the resuscitation and I was breathing normally, my mother turned to thank the stranger… and he was gone. She asked everyone who he was and where she could find him. No one knew him or had ever seen him before. This happened at a small summer camp. The only people there were parents on a Sunday visit with their children. *Who was he? Why was he there? Where did he go?*

The mystery of the NDE remained as I grew up to ignite a passion to understand states of transpersonal consciousness, to understand the forces of synchronistic experiences (SEs) that manifested a stranger in the right place at the right time to save my life. It was clear to me that the two were linked, even though I did not have the words to express it.

I was profoundly changed by the experience and felt "different" in a way I have difficulty describing. I am unafraid of death. Knowing there is a place of bliss to which I could go served me well in the years to come of family troubles and a difficult adolescence. I could withdraw into dreaming states of consciousness by recalling the bliss of the NDE. Entering that dreamy state was to develop into a master switch I could turn on and off as the years went by. There were times that it was all the comfort I had.

However, I felt protected somehow, and the fear of being seriously hurt was absent. The memory of someone synchronistically coming when I was in danger sustained my faith that I was not alone. I was connected to some other reality and no one could persuade me of anything different.

The eminent psychologist, Carl Jung, is the originator of the term *synchronicity*. He described it as "... meaningful coincidences between persons and events in which an emotional or symbolic connection cannot be explained by cause and effect." Jung literally hung out with physicists in the 1920s and the idea reportedly came to him during a dinner conversation with Albert Einstein. It soon became clear that these physicists, later to be known as some of the foundational minds that developed quantum theory, and Jung were thinking along the same lines.

Jung believed that SEs demonstrated there exists a unified level of reality... *an unus mundus*... that reflects a fusion of both inner and outer reality. Later, this thinking would connect to the works of the eminent quantum physicist, David Bohm, in his classic work, *Wholeness and the Implicate Order*. In it he theorized the idea of a unified world fabric, *a holographic world,* wherein we are all connected to one another.

Synchronicity, then, can be seen to reflect a "deeper, more holistic reality." Although SEs can be simply defined as "meaningful coincidences," the elements that compose them are "acausal." In other words, we are unable to understand them via a cause and effect explanation. As Jung put it, "Two events, one inner and one outer, connect *not* by virtue of one causing the other, but by a mutual reflection of a common meaning." Many go unnoticed in everyday life; some are bigger and are blatantly obvious.

Synchronicity and Major Life Transitions

Six years later, the psychological ground of nurture and warmth with a significant other that carried me through three of my high school years shifted, ending in acute pain and rejection. I packed a suitcase, and not knowing where I was going or how to get there with only a few small bills in my pocket, I walked out the back door.

A co-worker of my father's saw me on the road and offered me an airline ticket to where my father lived. Unbeknownst to my father's friend, that was a risky connection, but it provided a bridge to leave home. Without food, protection, or shelter, I ended up in a strange town, living on the beach.

I could have been hurt in myriad ways, but I was not. Like the stranger who saved my life in the lake, kind strangers stepped up and provided safety and help. When I was hungry, I was given food. When it got cold at night, others took me to sleep where it was warm. In the spring, using a false address, I put myself back in school and walked away with a diploma. Everything I needed came, without asking. I was not alone.

With nothing more than a pretty face, I got a job modeling for commercial ads. I met my husband-to-be and carved out a new life as his wife and gave birth to two extraordinary sons.

Transition II

Ten years later, the stable ground of my new life shifted. Once again I lived in a house shadowed by unfounded, violent, jealous rages. Literally running for my life this time, people I didn't know stepped up who had heard of the situation. They offered to shelter me and my young sons. Hidden away, I waited until I thought it had calmed down. Then, I bought airline tickets to a safe location thousands of miles away.

Standing in line to board our flight, two officers pulled us aside with a warrant for my arrest. I didn't understand, but I could guess who was behind it. I stood there holding the warrant in my hand not knowing what to do, dreading who would appear any moment. A stewardess stepped up to me. Was I boarding? I said I could not in a low voice. I couldn't move. She left. People moved around us. The next thing I knew the pilot of the plane hurried up as the last call to board came over the speaker. He asked to see the warrant, read it briefly, and said, "Your sons are not listed on this warrant. Do you want them to board?" I nodded yes, pushed the "master switch" to step out of the panic and pain, and spoke quickly and calmly to my sons, preparing them to leave without me. Suddenly, without a word, the officers moved back. I was free to board with my sons. *What happened?* All I know is that I was assisted. Unknown others had come to my aid, again. My faith that I am not alone was validated.

Teleological Synchronicity

Another ten years passed. We don't remember days; we remember moments. Perhaps the ones we remember most are moments wherein our Souls want us to take note as the next steps. I remember living in a cabin in the Sierra Mountains at a time when I was so burned-out I couldn't continue my counseling career. Four years of working with chronic schizophrenic patients while going to school and single parenting took all I had.

My entry to studying psychology was the works of Carl Jung. He was the only one who dared acknowledge the Soul. So I devoured his works and those of his followers to reorient myself as I listened to the wind in the pines to soothe my broken spirit, not knowing if I could continue, or what my career now called upon me to do.

One of the books that came, I don't remember how, was Jean Bolen's *The Tao of Psychology Synchronicity and the Self*. I recall reading the book from cover to cover in one gulp, then dancing around the cabin with it held to my breast laughing and crying. I had found home ground! Her book gave me an explanation for my intuitive grasp of my life, my perception of the world as I experienced it. I was not alone in a weirdness of connections I could not articulate since the childhood NDE.

Connecting the Dots

I started graduate school. Part of master's training to become a psychotherapist is concurrent individual counseling. There was a list in the office of therapists available to work with students. None were Jungians. I delayed contacting any on the list. The deadline grew steadily closer.

The progam director sent for me. "What is wrong with the list?" she asked. I said I wanted a Jungian therapist. She replied, "Do you have anyone in mind? I'll see what I can do." I said, "Jean Bolen," and she laughed! "Dream on," she said. "Dr. Bolen is out of your league." She ended with a curt, "Choose someone on the list by the end of the week."

When I have a strong feeling that what I ask for is "right" I have an internal sense of quiet while waiting… I trust that some way or another all the pieces will come together. Three days went by.

Two days left. I did the preposterous; I called Dr. Bolen's office, ready to ask the impossible, to speak to Dr. Bolen. Unexpectedly, Dr. Bolen answered. When I finally caught my breath, I gave her a brief account of my status as a student and the school requirement. I rushed on to tell her of my experience while reading her book. She listened politely, but told me, gently, that she did not take students as analysands, her patients work with her for years, and she had a long waiting list. She thanked me for thinking of her.

Still, I didn't call anyone on the school list.

Last day. I remained still inside. I could barely breathe or put one foot in front of the other, but I went to class.

A message came from the office: Call Dr. Bolen.

Dr. Bolen was as incredulous as I when she told me that morning one of her analysands was unexpectedly reassigned to New York. She had called everyone on her waiting list. Each had either begun with another analyst or had moved. She felt an intuitive impulse to work with me. I did not have the words to tell the program director that I felt powerful forces had moved to fulfill a major step of my Soul's purpose. A miraculous year followed as Dr. Bolen and I began the healing that was not only required, but needed. I learned that I had traveled a "non-ordinary path" and that my courage to leave potentially damaging circumstances with faith that I was not alone had saved my life, psychologically. In my end-of-analysis dream, I saw myself power up a steep incline where Dr. Bolen waited at the top to pull me to the summit. I waded through a mercurial pool to step out with a small vial of the transformational fluid, my contribution to the long line waiting on the earthen shelf on the other side.

Ten years after analysis with Dr. Bolen, I arrived at a familiar balk near the end of my doctoral journey. It was time to select a research study topic. As I listened to my peers talk about their topics, I met an inner wall. To graduate ABD (all but dissertation) began to loom large. My adviser called me in. (Sound familiar?) My research method and design courses were starting. "Your topic is...?"

We went over optional topics. None gave the signal I was waiting for. My adviser asked me what triggered my passion. I asked, "Could I design a study of synchronicity as connection with one's Soul and life purpose?" "Well," he said. "That is not quite acceptable for a doctoral study. Jung's Synchronicity and Soul are not scientifically proven concepts." However, there was a faculty member I could talk to about a more scientific approach that might give me the results I was after.

Enter Dr. Ron Valle. He spent many hours working with me on my topic. It manifested as *A Phenomenological Study of the Experience of Being Carried Along by a Series or Flow of Unforeseen Circumstances or Events Culminating in a Right and Desired Outcome.* Dr. Valle honored me by joining my dissertation committee. I was ecstatic! Everything I needed had come to propose this "non-scientific study."

First, I had to study quantum physics.

Synchronistically, therein lay the scientific knowledge that explained my life experience, that supported and changed the study to "scientifically acceptable." Bohm's *Wholeness and the Implicate Order* became my primary text. Others quickly followed. Science had caught up with the *Perennial Wisdom Knowledge of the Tao* in Dr. Bolen's book that depicted a model of life as I experienced it. Everything I needed to conduct the study was there.

The study was exciting and fulfilling, and the analysis was published in a text on phenomenological design. With gratitude for its beginning point, I dedicated the dissertation to Dr. Bolen. *Life-Path Flow* is the book that was born from the study.

D. Marie Hanson, Ph.D, research psychologist, scholar, and mentor derives great satisfaction from assisting doctoral students producing cutting-edge research on the elements of what it is to be human, and others "connecting the dots" between the realities of human experience and the Divine. Visit www.OuroborosWorks. com to discuss your Life-Path experiences on her blog.

A Message for Humanity

Wendy Isaac

THIS CHAPTER IS A LOVE LETTER WRITTEN TO YOU...
sent from my heart to yours.

Peace is all there IS, all there ever was, and all that ever shall be.
What you think and believe to be real and true,
Will soon cease to exist in your reality,
The illusionary myth of me and you.

All memories and beliefs riddled with residuals of separation,
Will dissolve into the ether without trepidation.
Humanity shall finally be free of sorrow and fear,
We will harmoniously exist as One. This is Truth, my dear.

I promise you, those who crave for the world
to be free of all heartache and pain,
You will never have to experience any derivatives of these again.

The transformation has already commenced,
Joyfully celebrate, as there is no turning back.
The collective of humanity has made the choice,
Free will of individuals shall no longer alter the course.

Peace is truly all there is, all there ever was, and all there ever shall be.

Dear Sweet Child, I so desire to speak with you: about you, your soul's journey, and the journey that humanity now begins together. Come, take a seat next to me, settle in, and when you are ready, open your mind and heart so that this soul can assist you during these ever-changing times. Today, dear one, the time has come for us to discuss the cathartic evolution that you and the human race are now embarking upon.

I have asked you here today so that I can bestow upon you clarity, comfort, and a greater understanding as to what is happening during this momentous time in history. I have been leaning in and listening very closely to the conversations you and your earthly companions are having. Your curiosity is peaking and you crave to know more.

As I listen in on your conversations, I know with all of my being that you and the ones you love are ready, excited, and anxiously awaiting all that lies before you. You sense that everything is changing – you feel it to your core. You curiously talk about the immense shifts that are happening, and it feels like everything around you is changing at the speed of sound.

You wonder why it feels like spiritual awakenings and discoveries of astonishing magnitudes are happening more quickly than ever before. You notice others embracing methods and teachings that were greatly rejected afore. How is it that now is the time when the desire to become an aware spiritual being is the heart-centered goal of so many? You feel people's resistance beginning to wane and you can feel the hearts and souls of millions wanting to know the Truth of who they truly are. You have an innate understanding that there is a spiritual awakening happening here on earth, yet you feel there is more to it and that the scope of your understanding does not reveal the whole picture to you. Your desire to know the whole story has become insatiable, and this is why it is time that we meet together now.

I am filled with excitement for this moment in time, as I get to share with you what is on this heart of mine. Lean in, my dear, and I will share in part with you one of the greatest stories to be told in the history of mankind since the inception of your creation.

* * *

There was a moment in time... did you feel it? That magnificent moment when a decision was made and instantaneously the will of man collided with Unconditional Love from beyond. Every being on earth was then launched into a dawn of awakening. I was jolted by the agreement made between humankind and the Divine, and I know you felt it, too. My calling, and the calling of those I serve with, changed forevermore on that day. And the commencement of the evolution of mankind that I once saw only on the brink of existence is now coming to fruition. I am beside myself with joy as it is a most amazing time in history for all of humanity.

This moment in time I speak of is the very instant that everything changed forevermore; the paradigm that commenced with the birth of the very first human to walk on this earth is now coming to an end. The collective journey of mankind in this time-and-space experience shall now have its final curtain call. What does this mean? What is really going on? The time has come, dear one... it is now time for "Humanity's Great Awakening."

There is so much to share, and we only have a short time together today. I will do my best to give you a peek into all that lies before you with the intention that it will give you clarity. What I am sharing today may fill you with excitement or leave you with some residual doubt or fear, but please know that my longing is to leave you feeling inspired and to bestow hope upon your heart and soul. Know that you are supported and loved for eternity, and that you are always held in the hearts and hands of God, the Divine, and all the amazing souls who serve in the most tender and loving ways. You are never alone.

The reality for humanity is now surpassing the imaginative and creative presentations of fiction as never before. Hold on tight... and let the journey begin.

It all started with a call, a desperate call for help that was sent out by you and humanity that was heard throughout the heavens and universe. Your call came to us in the form of prayers and pleas for there to be Peace on earth, and for your reality to be free of conflict, violence, poverty, greed, wars, and self-deprecation. You begged to be free of fear, pain, and sorrow. The call's urgency pierced the hearts and souls of every being that exists in all of creation.

We watched from beyond and craved to step in and assist you in every way possible, but the time had not come yet, so we did what we could to support you for the time being. We held you all in the highest vibration of Light, Love, and Truth possible, not only to comfort you, but with the conviction that you soon would be ready to move beyond the circumstances of your own creation. We patiently waited as we served you from beyond the veil and had high hopes that the tide would turn and we would be allowed to assist you in the way for which we were created. Our anticipation was palpable and we anxiously awaited the miracle so that we could fulfill our very own Divine callings.

Then, on the second-most-exciting day in human history since the day of earthly creation, the miracle happened and the mortal majority collectively decided that the course of mankind would shift for eternity. It was decided that it was time for humans to step into a new paradigm — a paradigm in which Peace and Love on earth would reign. Creation was rocked to the core the day that decision was made. Transition was set into motion and there would be no turning back. Even the free will of mankind would no longer alter the course. Souls were unbound and we could now serve you in a way in which we were never allowed to before. What lay ahead of us all, humankind and souls from beyond, would change history and launch you into all that your

70

hearts and souls desire, to live in Peace here on earth and to shift into a paradigm in which nothing except Love, Light, and Truth exists.

These are truly exciting times! The time has come, the time of your Human Awakening! You will be stepping into the most wonderful existence you have yet to live. You will be advancing into an awe-inspiring era that will liken to stepping into heaven on earth, and you will live a life filled with harmony, joy, and love to heights that you have never experienced before. I am so excited for all that awaits you! Soon you will awaken and live in a "Paradigm of Peace." It is now time to transcend the current paradigm of existence and usher in an era that is null and void of all that humanity craves to no longer be part of their reality... the illusionary reality of who you believe you are.

A collective Human Awakening? How in the world can this really happen, and how in the universe can this really be true — a time-and-space experience here on earth where there will be nothing except Peace and harmony across the entire globe? Yes this is not only possible, but will certainly come to pass. We promise. A Divinely orchestrated plan has already been created and has been set into motion. I see your heart fill with hope and excitement as you assimilate this probability, and yet there may also be uncertainty as to how something of this magnitude can really be true. You ask how you and others will have this Human Awakening. It will happen as you wake up to Truth... the Truth of who you truly are.

You are LIGHT, and you are LOVE,
And all that you believe the Divine and the Universe are~
IS who YOU are.

You individually are the creators of your experience.
When you realize this Truth and are in a full state of awakened
consciousness, YOU will then become ONE and undivided.
You shall live in Peace evermore.

Lean in a little closer, a little more than before, and I will share a secret with you... a secret that is only coming to the light of day in this very moment in time. I spoke of the agreement that was made between humans and the Divine – that day that shook creation to the core. It was on that very day that an insatiable desire began to burn in the hearts of our souls and we knew it was time for us to come forth and fulfill our magnificent calling. We were asked if we would be willing to serve in a new way here on earth, and be the first to assist you with your Great Awakening.

Yes, my dear, it is true. There are souls who once resided beyond the veil who are coming in to assist with this remarkable happening – souls who have been assisting you from the other side. We are your celestial guides who know you better than any other beings in all of creation. We are coming in because we love you so and because assisting you with your ultimate awakening is our calling. We are so honored and grateful beyond measure to step in and serve thee. We are beside ourselves with excitement because the day has come when Truth can now be heard, understood, digested, and assimilated as never before. Truly an astounding and brilliant time in history it IS!

I mentioned a plan that was orchestrated by the Divine, and before we part today I will give you a glimpse into how we will serve you during your incredible evolution. In summary, the following are highlights of what we will be focusing on:

- Foremost, we are here to teach and share Truth. We know the Truth, we speak the Truth, and we will teach the Truth in a way that can be easily understood and assimilated.

- We are here to help you wake up to the Truth of who we all are; to cut through the illusions and part the veil so the "real story" can be known.

72

• We will present you with easily applied methods, principles, and tools that will get you and the entire planet to Peace.

Rest assured that the methods, principles, and tools to get all humanity to Peace are easily understood. There will be nothing difficult to digest nor any huge learning curves involved. All it will take is your willingness to follow the path laid before you. You may be surprised that the information presented is nothing "new," as there is nothing new to introduce. All Truth you need to awaken has been presented in one form or another for centuries. The difference now is that everything you need to know will be presented in a way in which you will have all the information cohesively in hand and you will no longer need to piece together instructions to try to figure out the most effective path to Humanity's Great Awakening.

Each of us coming in has our own unique message and method for teaching Truth. I am currently working on the key message I am here to deliver and formulating a set of principles you can utilize. If you choose to participate, I promise you will get to Peace, and ultimately you will have your own awakening. All you have to do is believe and put the principles into practice. My heart soars knowing that soon you and I shall come together again and that I will be able to place into your heart and hands "The Principles of Peace."

Our time together, for the moment, must come to an end. I see you on the edge of your seat ready to learn and receive more. Trust that soon you will have even greater clarity with your own awakening.

Thank you, my dear sweet child, for allowing me to share this message with you today. I do hope you received clarity, comfort, and a greater understanding as to what is happening during these pivotal times, and that you are filled with hope that soon Peace will prevail.

As we part for today, I ask that you close your eyes and breathe in all the possibilities that are before you. Open your heart far and wide, and then allow the Truth to embrace you and set you free.

73

Until we meet again... know that the tide has turned. Let go and release all that you believed was true. Trust that the majority has chosen to head towards Peace. The resistance is waning and all you need to do now is turn towards the Light and ALLOW the loving flow of the Divine to assist you in transitioning into Peace and harmony. Feel the embrace of the Almighty and know that Peace on Earth, and Love, shall reign evermore.

Wendy's book, *The Principles of Peace,* is planned for release in 2016. She is an author, speaker, and teacher of Truth and has a degree in new thought and metaphysics. Wendy currently teaches, advocates, and mediates on behalf of peace and conducts workshops that assist and inspire individuals on their path to living joyful and harmonious lives. If you would like to speak with Wendy or receive information about her book, services, and speaking engagements, visit www. WendyIsaac.com.

The Journey

Michael James

RAISED IN A CHRISTIAN HOME, I felt like I lived at church and was there every time the doors were opened. I was there on Sunday morning, Sunday night, Saturday prayer night, and Wednesday kids' night. I went to the same church's private school until sixth grade. I didn't know anything else but things pertaining to hard-core Christianity. No, we weren't handling snakes, but there was a lot of running, yelling, speaking in tongues, and fear that if you did something wrong you would go to hell. I never had an option to go or not to go to church. It was part of my life. Going to church was no different from brushing my teeth: I did it whether I liked it or not.

When I was about eight years old, I had this lingering question running through my mind: "How is it that we are the only ones who have 'it' – the correct way to live according to Christians, right?" I started questioning my religious beliefs at an early age. "What about the Baptists? What about the Catholics, Methodists, Buddhists, and every other religion? How is it that we, the Pentecostals, which is a small denomination compared to many, have it right?"

Growing up was difficult with so many religious rules, a father who was a former marine, and having all these religious questions running through my mind. My siblings and I were raised with hard-core rules. We were not allowed to make mistakes, misbehave, or just be kids. We worked in our mom's craft business, had a rigorous chore list, and of course, went to church. There was no time to go outside to play and be a kid. The only time that was allowed was when my dad was not home, and sometimes I lied about a school project and rode my bicycle to a friend's house to hang out. Surrounded by strict rules within my home and at church, I grew up feeling that going to church and living that lifestyle was the only way to exist (even though I questioned it internally). Anything outside of that was contrary to how I was raised. So I stayed plugged into the church as I became an adult and tried to obey all the rules that Christianity pushed on a person's life.

At twenty-one, I married a Christian girl and we quickly got involved in a church and did all the "right" things. I was always striving for more, but never obtained anything. I would give sacrificially, but it never seemed to come back my way. I couldn't understand. I was doing everything right. I was at church every time the doors were opened and volunteered for everything that needed to be done. My wife and I went on mission trips and later spent two years living in Peru helping with the church youth group, teaching English, building a school, being translators for medical teams, and raising our son in a foreign country. Again, I was doing everything "right."

After our two years' living in Peru, we felt it was time to come home. I picked up where I had left off with my business and quickly started back living an American lifestyle. For me that included getting plugged back into the church where we were previously members. This time around, something wasn't right. My wife was going through a hard time and the church wasn't there for her as we had been taught it would be. I kept pushing through and was always optimistic about things getting better.

We soon had our second child, but shortly after she was born I lost my mother, who was a devout Christian. After her death, those childhood questions started circling back in my head. "How is it that we Christians are the only ones who have it right?" My world slowly started crumbling. Within a year, my wife came to me and said that she was now an atheist and no longer believed in what we, as a couple, had spent the last ten years believing. I was absolutely crushed! I didn't know what to do with my emotions, so I suppressed them and acted like nothing had happened.

My marriage started to fall apart in so many ways. I was lost and felt that everything I had been taught was null and void. Within two years I was signing divorce papers. Not knowing what to do, within months I jumped into a relationship that quickly became rocky. I struggled with anxiety and a lack of awareness about what was going on within me. At the time I had just started racing my bicycle and felt that was the only relief I had from all my worries. I would ride my bicycle all the time… for hours, every day. It quickly became a fix to the emotional drama that was unfolding in my life.

By the time another two years had gone by, I had remarried and divorced for the second time. I felt like a total failure. But the one thing I was not a failure at was riding my bicycle. At this point in my life, I had pretty much lost everything I had, including my self-confidence. I had given up on going to church and felt like it was only a place to go and be judged by others for my failures. My only solitude from judgment was riding and racing my bicycle, which I happened to be good at. I didn't realize it at the time, but I was slowly being exposed to a self-development side of myself that the "church" did not provide. However, I was still experiencing a rollercoaster of emotions. I was in another relationship that I had no business being in and I knew I had to make a change! I couldn't keep going like I was going.

In January of 2012, I decided I was going to train and ride my bicycle across the United States. I bought a one-way ticket to San Francisco, California. That ticket propelled me into a commitment that has changed my life forever. I planned for a start date of June 3rd. I made a little poster of the map of the United States and the route I was going to take on my journey. I filled it with positive statements and hung it on my wall to see daily. Meanwhile I trained, trained, and trained. I would ride twenty-five to thirty-five miles every weekday and on Saturday's ride one hundred miles. Sundays I would ride another hundred miles pulling a bicycle trailer full of rocks to simulate the weight that I would be pulling on the trip.

Things were coming together as friends, family, and individuals started hearing about my future trip. A local bike shop sold me supplies at cost, a sports clothing company gave me clothing, and a bicycle company gave me a bike. I was set and ready to go. After months of training and hundreds of miles under my belt thus far, the day finally arrived. I packed my bike and supplies and flew to San Francisco to start this journey.

What the Hell?

Waking up in my tent on the third morning of my trip, I had already completed one hundred and seventy miles. I was lying there looking at the rooftop of my tent when I said to myself, "What the hell am I doing?" By day number three I was tired, the newness of the trip had worn off, and I was second-guessing my commitment. With some thoughts of backing out in my mind, I was quickly reminded of the commitment I had made to myself and got ready for my day of cycling and moving closer to my destination.

Spinning My Wheels

Throughout the next couple of days, I faced a lot of mental struggles which became my hardest obstacle to overcome. As I crossed over into Nevada from California, the landscape changed a bit and I found myself climbing a mountain and then descending into a long, flat valley. It would then be twenty to forty miles to the next mountain range. Approaching cars looked like little dots off into the distance. Day after day the landscape was the same. I felt as if I was spinning my wheels getting nowhere fast. I was putting so much effort into my ride and the miles were ticking away, but emotionally I felt I was going nowhere. Up the mountain, down the mountain, and into the valley for hours on end only to ascend the next mountain. Every day that went by felt like mental torture. Physically speaking, I was strong as an ox, never having any issues at all; yet mentally I was breaking down by the minute.

Temper Tantrum

A couple of days later, I stopped at a local diner after riding fifty miles. I had to make a decision to continue to the next town, which was seventy miles away with a huge mountain to climb, or stay the night where I was. I finished lunch and decided to continue, although I knew this would be difficult. Hour after hour passed ascending this mountain. I felt like I was never going to make it to the top. Darkness was falling when I finally made it to the top of the mountain and started my descent. I knew I was not going to make it to the next town, which now was thirty-five miles away. Off in the distance was a very familiar sight: a long, straight, flat road... miles to the other side. I could barely see the outline of a house four or five miles away. I thought if I could make it there I could ask to camp in their yard and ask for some fresh drinking water.

As the sun descended and I was trying my best to get to this house, I got a flat tire. I became so frustrated and angry trying to change the tire that I was having a good old temper tantrum. I mean I was kicking my bike, kicking the grass, and getting very emotional. After calming down, I got the tire changed and made my way to the house where a sweet old lady allowed me to camp in her yard and filled up my water bottles. At this point, I knew it was time for a physical and mental break. The next morning I rode thirty miles to a small town and rented a hotel room to take a much-needed break.

I felt amazing after a full day of doing nothing but eating, lying in bed, and getting refocused on this cross country journey. The next day it was time to get on the bike and just pedal. Days went by with minor problems, mostly just flat tires. I averaged a flat tire every day. Finally, biking through Nevada and Utah was over and I moved on to the more difficult climbing I had yet to face.

The Crash

I was caught up in an extremely long climb up to Lizard Head Pass and looking forward to a fifteen-mile descent into Telluride, Colorado. The sweeping road as I descended from left to right felt like freedom. A mile from town, traffic became heavy due to a festival in Telluride. I was aware of the cars behind and in front of me, so to be safe I slowed down – only to find myself veering off the road to avoid debris and potholes. The sand and gravel roadside didn't help and I started losing control of my bicycle. The wheels slid out from underneath me. I tumbled and hit the side of an embankment, falling into a creek twenty feet from the road... then silence.

Suddenly I woke up. What had happened? "Where is the fire?" I thought to myself, as a firefighter helped me climb up to the road where I found myself surrounded by paramedics and onlookers. All I could think about was my trip and just pedaling. However, my bike was in bad shape, my body was in pain, and now I really faced the thought of quitting. The only thing I could think of was to call my brother. His words would be an encouragement regardless of the decision I had to make. Not only were they reassuring, but he kept saying, "Just keep pedaling! If you don't get back on your bike it will be harder every day that passes." Early the next day, I rose with a sore body and started pedaling. Within three days, all the soreness had subsided and I was back in the groove.

I Had Enough

On day number thirty-nine, I had made it to the North Carolina state line. I only had four days of riding left before I would make it to Onslow Beach, North Carolina. At that point my body was physically exhausted. I was starting to see the light at the end of the tunnel, but my mind was taking me to another place. I was ready to quit. I was prepared to rent a car and drive the last four hundred miles. I was trying to convince myself that I had ridden from California to North Carolina and that was enough. Nobody had to know that I hadn't gone all the way to the coast. I could just tell people that I rode my bicycle from California to North Carolina... even though I was barely over the state line. Yet my integrity would not allow it. I had made a commitment and was going to follow through.

As I made it to the coast and was welcomed home by so many people, I couldn't help but desire to be on my bicycle. Those next few days were extremely hard. As physically demanding as the trip had been, I had done something that had changed my life.

The Aftermath

Three years later, as I'm writing this chapter, I realize that the important thing wasn't the trip or the goal of cycling thirty-five hundred miles in forty-two days, but the actual journey itself. Our lives are nothing more than a journey. Everything that has happened up to this point is part of our journey. We will have what-the-hell moments, experience spinning our wheels, and have temper tantrums and crashes, but the key to making it through all of these obstacles is to keep pedaling. All the things that happened to me as a kid, my relationships, my life, is just a simple journey. Opportunities are made, relationships are developed, and a story is created.

So... what is *your* story? What is *your* journey?

Michael James, a business owner, success coach, and motivational speaker, inspires people from all walks of life to embrace their journey and experience the life of their dreams. The lessons he learned bicycling solo across the country for forty-two days caused life-changing shifts that led to a 400 percent growth of his construction company, a newfound enthusiasm for life, and a new career coaching and mentoring people to accomplish their dreams while enjoying the journey. Michael@ShiftingYourMindset.com

True North:
On Truth, Trust, and Love

Steven Lovink

IF THERE EVER WAS A TIME POISED for limitless possibilities of transformation of self and society, it must be *now*. The suspense is affecting all of humanity — you and me — in both subtle and not-so-subtle ways. It is as if the universe is pulling us back as one into the only direction that creates, regenerates, and fulfills potential. It has the backs of those who embrace what has always been the True North of an interconnected, ever-expanding universe — not unlike a persistent siren's call to align our higher selves in matters small and large with the propelling energies of a compass course pointing to truth, trust, and love.

Some of us will choose to remain entangled in trauma or drama relating to the past, present, and/or future. This really means we cannot be found at home — *in the now*. It is for this reason that our purposeful, deeply caring universe will nudge, with force or even occasional deep discomfort, those who linger in absence too long, avoiding presence, to serve our evolution. Where truth, trust, and love (as in surrender to universal love) no longer reign, a lack of care creates the future. Beautiful relations can no longer emerge, grow, mature, and sustain life. You can think of this in terms of relations among partisans – people, couples, businesses, and governments – as opposed to partners in life mirrored through a frayed web of relations with nature on the only planet we have.

Can you see that the "whole of life" has been withering away on a course deviating from True North? Do you feel how the quality of our individual and collective relations reflects this reality? This is why we must contemplate often whether our lives are heading True North and whether we love ourselves enough to not only attract true love, but also to love others as ourselves, as well as the Earth, as one.

Two days after the traumatizing Paris terrorist attacks in November of 2015, I attended a beautiful concert for orchestra and choir in the Cathédrale Saint Cécile in Albi, France. This ancient episcopal town is a UNESCO world heritage site. You easily find yourself feeling as if you've been transported back to the Middle Ages. It is here where the legend of Sainte Cécile took hold. She did not favor marriage, heard and sang celestial songs from her heart, and was eventually boiled to death by a Roman prefect irritated by the gossip around town. Eventually Cécile was sanctified, became known as the patron of musicians, and is now remembered every year with a mesmerizing concert.

The *curie* of Cathédrale Saint Cécile invited an audience of a thousand or more from all walks of life and belief systems to join him in a moment of silence honoring the victims and families of the Paris attacks. He reminded everyone of the dual reality that "force" could be both malevolent and benevolent. The Paris attacks represented the former and the security forces at the entrance of the cathedral symbolized the latter as flip sides of the same coin. The *curie* then proceeded to invite us to reach beyond this powerful, polarizing event and the institutionalized confines of his church – even all of Christianity – by reminding us that *the greatest force of all is love,* for love is what unifies all of humanity as *one* in all of its diversity. It was as if he was saying, in the words of the poet Rumi, "Out beyond ideas of wrongdoing and right doing there is a field," and we were all invited to meet there. Precious moments of silence ensued, creating a unified field of consciousness later amplified and deeply resonating with a concert reminiscent of the celestial songs Cécile once heard.

If the *curie's* message feels somewhat heretical to you that thought would not be totally out of place, for Albi is a region of France known for Catharism (a dualistic theology), which is still practiced today. Knights Templar once roamed the fields there. Toulouse-Lautrec lived and painted in Albi as well. And so it is that faith, legend, lore, and the Paris attacks fused to forever seal the past, present, and future of Albi with that of Paris *in the now* on that day — a fusion of realities across space-time and multiple dimensions occurring all at once, simultaneously as one.

A portion of this chapter was written the day after winter solstice, a moment of the year when stillness and movement are said to play together as one. It is a precious time capsule, vessel, or chalice from which everything arises and to which everything returns — a moment frozen in the revelation of timelessness: just after Thanksgiving when most US families celebrate the abundance of the land and life and reunite with loved ones; just before universally unifying traditions and their messages of love and peace flood our hearts during a worldwide holiday season; and just before the dawning of the celebratory start of a newly birthed year. It is somehow a period of eternal times memorial, during which we can feel, tap into if you like, an alchemical fusion of three other parallel universes: a shared historical human past fraught with only partially understood trauma; a present existence or global being mirroring humanity's great, yet illusionary challenge of separation; and a palpable, expansive future pregnant with creative solutions and unbound by any limits on those solutions. Yes, change is coming upon us at an extraordinary, exponential, persistent pace. There can be no driving into our future from the rear view mirror, as one is bound to hit even the last standing tree, crash, and burn. We must navigate the future *now*, from the core of our hearts, and instantaneously. A busy mind always offers too little too late when extraordinary change is exponential. It is from this truth, and trust and love that we must seek to evolve the world and ourselves. Are we ready to wake up, head True North, and evolve?

If you have any doubts about whether our world is changing fast, or the imperative of all of us plugging in and playing big with each other, then consider what Brazilian new-economy entrepreneur Gustavo Tanaka experiences as being at the core of something extraordinary happening in our world. I am paraphrasing his eight elements of the core and building on them below:

- *The broken employment model* — Greater numbers of people drop out of big corporations, government, or otherwise seemingly secure organizations, or leave on sabbaticals, suffer from work-related depression, and burn out. Their futures seem to be elsewhere. More people are willing to risk everything to become entrepreneurs — artisans of a new world — to find and fulfill their life's purpose.

- *The changing entrepreneurial model* — For decades entrepreneurs have been transforming their homes and garages into offices, if not labs, to launch billion-dollar solutions. But the search for funding one's venture, entrepreneurial dreams, and life purpose tends to be corrupted by a prevailing business investment model with money as its primary driver. Entrepreneurs end up as employees of their own creations, beholden to their financial backers. But a new type of purpose-driven evolutionary entrepreneur has been emerging. They are committed to operating and funding their businesses in more generative ways for the mutual benefit of the whole of society and their own ability to flourish sustainably.

- *The rise of collaboration* — The wisdom and logic of the sharing, collaborative economy — as opposed to the each-person-for-him/herself, competitive economic model designed to ensure the survival of the fittest — is quickly catching on. Sharing is caring, while building relationships, community, and greater purpose through collaboration.

- *The power of the Internet* — The greatest legacy of the Internet may well be its ability to give a potential voice to everyone. Humanity is now largely wired and wirelessly interconnected to information and people we want and need, beyond the control of big media or government. The Internet is bringing our world together in community, and contains the seeds of transforming a dated control system that no longer serves humankind effectively.

- *The emerging conscious consumer* — Do we really need to buy all the new and latest things we are supposed to want, wear, and have? More and more people are discovering less is more, as is sharing a car, office, or house. They vote with their pocketbooks. Companies and shareholders invested in conspicuous consumption must respond, face loss, or worse. The growing market opportunity is to serve those living better with fewer possessions.

- *The food system's transformation* — We become what we eat and are rediscovering the importance of eating healthy, nutritious food. Our changing habits and consumption patterns are transforming a global food system that is no longer secure, resilient, or healthy. Small farmers, as well as communities in urban and regional settings, are becoming increasingly relevant to the chain of production and distribution of food. This is transforming local and global economies by leaps and bounds as a whole system comes together to nourish our bodies consciously and well.

- *The awakening of spirituality* — The perception that spirituality is only for esoteric persons, weirdos, and mystics has long been surpassed by the reality of many of our friends, neighbors, and colleagues engaging in yoga and meditation at home, work, or school. Beyond reason and rationality there is something else going on, and we want to understand and feel it. In Gustavo's words: "You want to understand how these things work. How life operates, what happens after death, what is this energy thing people talk about so much, what is quantum physics, how thoughts can be materialized and create our sense of reality, what is coincidence and synchronicity, why meditation works, how is it possible to cure using nothing but bare hands, how those alternative therapies not approved by traditional medicine can actually work." And so human consciousness expands as more of us search and find answers within.

- *The liberation of education* — Does our educational system really prepare us for the future that lies ahead, or are we teaching from the rear view mirror, trying to preserve the status quo of a dated system, breeding just ordinary human beings rather than unleashing their greatest potential? Why is it that more people are working hard to rethink education through concepts like unschooling, back-schooling, homeschooling, whole-brain literacy, and being limitless? How many of us are being taught to keep our internal compass pointed to True North and live in harmony with nature and the universal laws of the cosmos — the core curriculum for a unifying university of life? Information, knowledge, educators, teachers, facilitators, best-of-class content, even experiential knowing of the whole of life is increasingly accessible everywhere and anytime to satisfy the curiosity and synchronize even the most hungry hearts and minds. It will change everything, and is already doing so now.

So yes, something extraordinary is happening in our world indeed. Yet the many ways in which individuals and humanity as a whole continue to live mostly separated from truth, trust, and love are as remarkable as they are unfortunate. How can we be unshackled from limiting belief systems and set sail more easily on a compass pointing to True North?

I personally believe that the answer lies in what one might describe as a better understanding of the alchemy of money, love, and life. To put it simply, we must become deeply aware of whether and how our money system is organized to infuse the whole of life with love and integrate indigenous principles of reciprocity, respect, responsibility, and relationships. Our current money system does not work that way and it has kept humanity confined to repetitive cycles of the trauma and drama of past, present, and future entanglements. We mostly pursue money for money's sake. Its negative consequences can be discerned all around us. Our money system must thus be reconfigured so that money flows in (is gifted and invested in) regenerative directions that enable us to realize a peaceful, sustainable, and prosperous future beyond our wildest expectations. There is really no reason why this cannot become our reality now, and it is slowly beginning to take shape. I believe it will eventually create a rapidly expanding ecosystem of whole-system entrepreneurs committed to starting "living businesses" generating and reinvesting what I call *Profits4Life,* jumpstarted with gifts. It is a generative entrepreneurial model reciprocating what we are all endowed with individually, collectively, and by the Earth when we are born to become responsible world stewards respecting all our relations. I must leave you hanging in regard to Profits4Life, for lack of space, but you can read more about it on my website listed below.

The transformation of self and the transformation of society are mirror images of the micro and macro constellations of life. Societies cannot change but for what transforms within the people who populate them. Collective transformation at scale will not easily happen unless a certain tipping point is reached in the aggregate. Coincidence and harmony increase as our individual consciousnesses reach frequencies that synchronize with those of likeminded hearts and minds. But that synchronicity may still be insufficient to reach the desired societal tipping point. Much is in play, always.

My own transformational journey continues, as does the homework it demands. As I write the final words of this chapter, I am emerging from a period some call a "dark night of the soul." I had tried to sustain a thirty-year-long marital relationship that was insufficiently supported by mutual reciprocity, respect, and responsibility. It was built on the quicksand of what I came to understand was non-integrated past trauma corrupting truth, trust, and love. It kept me increasingly distant from what we perceived to be our own version of True North as years went by. The resolution is ending up being the dissolution of a love that could not grow, change, or transform, at least not as a couple. I believe our separation is setting us free and is the most loving option to see through to its fruition. The truth of it all has forced me to suspend all judgment, surrender, trust the outcome, and continue to love with compassion. The life lesson I am learning is that to be able to fulfill my purpose in life and experience true unconditional and universal love, my compassion and love of self has to at least be equal to the compassion I have for others and the world. And so it is that my past, present, and future are being untangled in the now. It felt as though I needed to pry up a huge stone to open up the necessary breathing space to fully create from this point henceforth.

As I emerge from this life-changing reality, I catch glimpses of limitless possibilities, not the least of which is to share with others my transformational story and vision for the individual and collective human journey ahead. I sense that my personal quest is releasing gifts that, dare I say, may inspire many to help manifest the reality of a peaceful, sustainable, and prospering way of life by 2025.

Won't you meet me then, there, and in the unifying field along the way?

Steven Lovink is a visionary entrepreneur, peace-builder, whole-system thinker, and outside-of-the-box change-maker. Committed to building wholes greater than the sums of their parts, he continues his life's journey sensing humanity's emerging future and assembling its building blocks a piece at a time. He is currently working on his forthcoming book, provisionally titled *On Profits4Life — The Alchemy of Money, Love, and Life*. For more information visit www.lovink.life.

Hopeful Entry – My Beginning Journey of Faith, Hope, Love, and Determination

Veronica R. Lynch, Ph.D.

HAVE YOU EVER BEEN SO DETERMINED to create your own life's journey from surviving to thriving that you would choose to rely on faith and watch things work for your greater good? Well, I did. I was so tired of wearing a face of anger, shame, disappointment, and abandonment after the loss of my mom and my homeland, that I knew I needed to create more peace and joy in my life.

My biggest goal at that time was to get a college education that would prepare me to help myself and others. I desperately wanted to minimize the sadness and loneliness that can accompany fear, grief, and abandonment for many people, and help them learn how to better cope with life.

When I was eight years old, my mother migrated from our native island, Antigua, to St. Thomas in search of a better life. When I was ten years old, she sent for me and my younger brother, and we were able to get on her work bond in order to attend school in St. Thomas.

Two years later, due to mom's illness, she, my brother, and I had to return to Antigua. After only two months in Antigua, my mother died.

After her death, I returned to St. Thomas to live with my sister and her family. At that time I was granted a school bond that would expire upon my high school graduation.

Now that I was seventeen, it would soon be time for me to make my way in creating my own fulfilling lifestyle. I would have to leave the island and the guardianship of my sister and her family because the law only allowed you to stay there on a school bond until your high school graduation, and mine was quickly approaching. I had prepared myself by obtaining excellent clerical skills to fall back on if I couldn't create something else to sustain me along my life's journey.

Each day of the last two weeks of high school was a day of excitement and a sense of completion for my graduating classmates, while my excitement was shrouded by nerve-wracking anticipation and fear rapidly encroaching upon my psyche. The immigration authorities would be coming to deport me to my home island where there was no one there to receive me. I needed to believe my Higher Power would be there at my beck and call to provide for my needs while I pursued my heart's desire. I had to totally trust in this belief. Yet I first had to depend on friends and family to get me to a safe place to stay so I wouldn't be deported.

My escape route began on St. Thomas, United States Virgin Islands, the third day after my high school graduation. My teenaged heart filled with fear when someone pounded on the door of our island home at two o'clock in the morning. "Immigration!" shouted a voice from outside the door. The immigration authorities made a habit of showing up at people's homes unannounced at the moment their bond or legal documents expired. Those who didn't have legal status were constantly in fear and were harassed. It was common to hear the loud banging of the officers pounding on doors and people screaming, running, and trying to get away from the authorities for fear that they would be deported or sent to jail.

In her Caribbean dialect, my sister yelled, "Hol' on, hol' on," as she hurriedly threw a tattered bathrobe over her nightclothes and headed for the door.

I heard the ruckus, but was paralyzed with fear when my uncle ran into my room and pulled me out of bed while barely audibly whispering, "Quick, girl, put on your clothes and jump out the window. Immigration is at the door! You must run to Miss Ella's house. She will know what to do." I was scurrying about in the dark to find and put on the clothes I had on the day before, when my uncle handed me a suitcase that had already been packed in preparation of the authorities' arrival. In my haste I forgot to put on my shoes, but I continued to jump out the window into the night and raced down Mango Road, leaving loud voices of anger and authority behind me.

There were no street lights to guide me through the darkness, but I ran as fast as I could through the alleyways and high bushes. My bare feet began to ache from the sharp rocks I encountered as I ran for my life. With tears streaming down my face, I finally arrived at Miss Ella's door, praying that she would receive me at that time of the night. As soon as she opened the door I fell into her arms and continued to weep from fear.

Miss Ella, a native of St. Thomas, had not only bonded my mother and sister as housekeepers for her and her family, but she had always been a supportive friend to my mother.

"Lord, chil', you made it," Miss Ella cried in her Caribbean dialect, holding me firmly in her arms. In a calm, welcoming voice she whispered, "You're safe now." She grabbed my suitcase and helped me into her house. Though her pleasant face showed signs of relief, she looked tired and sleepy and I was embarrassed because I felt I was disturbing and burdening her.

She fixed me a cup of peppermint bush tea, but fear was shaking my body so much I couldn't hold the cup steady. "You must keep up your strength," she said, pulling up a chair to sit closer to me. "Drink, chil'," she insisted, putting the china teacup to my mouth. "It will make you feel better."

Miss Ella didn't seem too surprised at my showing up on her doorstep, and from the tone of her voice and actions, she had been expecting it to happen — it was just a matter of when. "You're a strong girl," she said. I didn't feel strong. I felt afraid, dependent on others, and unsure of my future. I had arrived at her home in the middle of the night, my dress sweaty and ripped, and before sunrise I had awakened her out of her sleep.

"No worry, babe. Everything is going to be alright," she said as she put her arm around me and gave me one of her nightgowns to put on. Just then she noticed my swollen, bloody feet. She quickly brought in a basin filled with warm water, poured the antiseptic Dettol in it, and began washing my feet. After drying them and applying aloe vera gel, she said, "This will help with the healing."

I trusted Miss Ella and she trusted me. When I was fourteen years old, Miss Ella had allowed me to work in her mother's home and in her apothecary after school. I would often sit and read the philosophical books in her library which fed my quest for learning. She always encouraged me to pursue an education.

After drinking the tea, I felt a little calmer, yet very tired. I looked at the clock. By now it was about 5:00am, so I decided to close my eyes for a second. I must have fallen asleep because when I woke up it was dark again. I felt disoriented and didn't know where I was. Looking about the room, I saw books in a tall bookcase and pictures of Miss Ella's son and her husband. Her husband was a military man and stationed in the United States. These things helped to ground me and recognize where I was.

It was now 5:00pm, and I wanted to get up and look for my clothes when I realized that there was still a dull ache in both my feet, though the swelling had gone down. I managed to make it across the room and opened my suitcase to see if my graduation picture was there, but it was not. I started remembering how proud I had felt walking down the aisle at Charlotte Amalie High School less than a week before to receive my high school diploma.

"I'm glad you're awake," Miss Ella said, entering the room with my clothes. She'd washed and sewn up my dress. "You're a brave girl. Your life is about to be transformed." Inside I did not feel brave. It was the summer of 1977 and graduation had come and gone. My school bond had expired at midnight on graduation day and I had no definitive plans as to what I would be doing with my life.

"I know you're hungry by now," Miss Ella smiled. "Yes," I whispered, and tried to return her smile. "Me soon come back," she said in her native dialect as she briskly left the room. "Okay," I replied, smelling my freshly cleaned clothes as I began to put them on.

Miss Ella returned shortly thereafter with a tray of food and stood in the doorway. With a smile she said, "You're not going to need clothes right now. It's almost time to go back to bed." So I took off my clothes and replaced them with Miss Ella's nightgown once more. I quickly ate the stewed fish with peas and rice she had prepared and brought to me.

I learned from Miss Ella that my sister had left a message earlier and would be visiting me the next day. "How are your feet doing?" she inquired. "Let me see them." She noticed that the swelling had left my feet so she massaged them with cocoa butter.

I awoke the next day eagerly anticipating seeing my sister. She came during her lunch hour and brought a package for me. Among the things my sister brought to me were my shoes, my high school diploma, a notebook, and my unframed graduation picture. In the package was a separate manila envelope in which was an airline ticket to Puerto Rico en route to New York City. She informed me that I would not be returning to my home in St. Thomas, but would be leaving for the US that night. She then pressed $200 into my hands, more money than I had ever seen at once. She was not able to stay long because she had just started a new job at the local bank and did not want to return late. We said our goodbyes quickly as we hugged and cried.

For the next few hours Miss Ella and I talked about my goals and dreams as I prepared for the trip. Before I knew it, I was in Miss Ella's car and we were speeding to the airport. My heart was beating so hard it felt as if it would burst through my chest at any minute. I felt torn because I would be leaving my home, yet I realized it was time for my escape. I had little time to say goodbye to Miss Ella, who hurriedly checked me in at the gate. Sitting in the airport while waiting to board the flight was not exactly fun-filled for me. I was too afraid that my secret of escaping would be discovered.

Approximately two hours later I boarded a six-seat plane for the short flight to Puerto Rico. Upon arrival, the airline attendants announced there would be a delay. I had no way of letting my family in the States know of the delay, so I began to worry. I sat quietly for about two hours until they announced that the next 747 jumbo jet heading for JFK airport in New York City would be boarding shortly. Miss Ella had already told me that "red eye" flights were the best time to travel because you're less conspicuous. My instructions were to board the jumbo jet heading for the States to begin my new life.

Once in the plane, when the attendants announced over the loudspeakers that we would be taking off shortly and to fasten our seatbelts, multiple emotions enveloped me. I felt sad, alone, and displaced because I was leaving behind my sister and St. Thomas, the place that had become my home after my mother's death. Yet at the same time I felt excitement because I was going to meet my two older sisters in the States, who had immigrated there five years prior. I felt fear because I was going to a place I had never been before, and I didn't know what to expect or even if I would like it. I also felt concern about my legal status. In addition, I was not sure which of my sisters I'd be staying with when I arrived in New York. When the jet started moving and lifted off the tarmac, I looked out my window and could see the lights of Puerto Rico getting smaller in the distance. I started praying and thanking God. This was the point of no return.

My feet were beginning to burn so I removed my shoes. I must have fallen asleep because the next thing I knew they were announcing we would be landing soon. My anxiety immediately increased and my hands began to sweat when a man in an official-looking uniform walked down the aisle. I held my breath and felt relief after he passed my seat.

I looked out the window in hopes that no one would discover me, and saw the vastness of the bright, colorful lights like a never-ending quilt below me. I took time to reflect on the words of Miss Ella and my sister. They both believed in me and encouraged me to believe in myself and stay focused and dedicated to my goals and aspirations. They knew I had the potential to create a life of empowerment and reminded me that prayer changes things. I had to rely on the God Source with which I was familiar from the foundation that my mom laid for me as a child. Again, having strong faith and belief in a Higher Power would be my source of survival.

I was ready to accept that I was strong, brave, and courageous, and could take on the challenge of creating the peaceful, blissful life I wanted through persistency, consistency, and determination. It would take another thirty-plus years before I finally shed my fear of deportation.

Healing artist **Veronica R. Lynch, Ph.D.,** empowers others to free themselves of the blocks from the past that prevent them from experiencing a life of abundance, peace, joy, happiness, and bliss. Veronica is co-author of the international bestselling book *Pebbles in the Pond — Wave 4*. Her book *Silent No More* is planned for release in 2016. For information about the book, visit www.VeronicaRLynch.com. For information about Veronica's retreats, products, and services, visit www.CreateWhole.com.

Stepping into My Authentic, Abundant, and Powerful Self

Beth Ellen Nash

ON THE OUTSIDE, I LOOKED LIKE I HAD it all together in high school. I led Bible studies and youth group, sang on worship teams, and even had the title "Missions Director." I wrote and directed our church's Christmas musical. I was honor society president and student council vice-president. I went to state in forensics. I was acting and assistant directing in my high school's musical. I was on my way to valedictorian with over a 4.0 GPA.

Inside, I was a disaster. This impressive litany of overachievement was simply my facade in order to prove my value and worth.

This "imposter-self" dissolved into tears many evenings on the drive home. I learned that if I forced the tears into submission by the time I got to the second-to-last house on the third block, I could paste the happy face back on and shallowly babble on about my various activities with my parents when I got home.

Behind closed doors, with the music turned up, I could break apart again. In my conservative Christian world there weren't acceptable outlets for doubt, depression, and anxiety. My parents couldn't model healthy ways to deal with emotions.

Journaling was my only tool for trying to process, and it wasn't enough. My mind often turned to a bottle of pills as a way out. One night that call was frighteningly loud. I called my best friend because I didn't want to die, but I could think of nothing else. She made me promise to see her in the morning. God used the story my friend wrote for me to plant the seed of hope and vision that I had a message and a purpose that needed to be shared with the world.

The story moved between two friends in high school and a distant tribe watching an eagle soaring overhead, eagerly awaiting its message. Back at the high school, an overdose claimed one of the girls' lives. Simultaneously, the tribe discovered the dead body of the eagle and mourned over a message that would never be heard.

Neither of us could have imagined that twenty-four years later a soaring eagle would be my logo for Wings to Soar Online Academy, the school I founded, where part of my tribe are dyslexics and other outside-the-box learners. Part of my message is breaking the chains of shame, failure, and inadequacy far too often associated with learning struggles.

I am breaking the silence as I tell my own story of being a highly sensitive person who has overcome the shame of childhood sexual abuse and who has broken out of allowing depression and anxiety to define me. I invite other women on the journey into wholeness to come with me.

Three Weeks of Unexpected Transformations

When I attended what I thought would be a series of business conferences, I had no idea about the transformative healing God had waiting for me. I had decided to invest in top-notch business mentors and surround myself with abundance-minded entrepreneurs, but I was not expecting the "Divine Appointments" God would provide so that I could begin to stand in my value and charge what I'm worth.

I arrived at Christine Kloser's Transformational Author Breakthrough exhausted from four months of sixty-five to eighty-five hour work weeks. I was focused on the word *author* as a means to professional publication. However, the transformational breakthrough I experienced as I went from tight, closed, and guarded on Monday morning to confidently declaring my new commitment to publishing my book, *Dyslexia Outside-the-Box,* as part of Christine's yearlong MasterHeart program, was beyond my wildest dreams. I knew that joining this program was going to force me to face my insecurities, sharpen every business skill I had, and dare me to declare my worth and expertise to the world.

Near the end of the three-week whirlwind of conferences, Ted McGrath powerfully modeled vulnerability and authenticity as he shared his own story in his show *Good Enough.* Inadequacies deep at my core bubbled to the surface, endangering my tender declaration.

The recurring night terrors surrounding my innate and complete defectiveness woke me with a crashing wave of shameful memories, followed by another wave of failure, and another of hopelessness. They threatened to drown my waking hours, but God stepped in through Coach Marc. I bravely asked the question during a group coaching session: "How am I supposed to stand in my value, charge what I'm worth, play a bigger game, and offer my gift to the world if at my core I still feel worthless?"

Coach Marc put his arm around me and let me shrink into my shawl, sobbing. Then he offered to lead me through a process of healing that would allow me to let go of this burden forever.

The imposter-self of perfection I had constructed in my childhood was fighting for her life. I wrestled for hours with the decision to invest in myself and trust the Divine Appointment God was offering me. I finally surrendered to allowing Coach Marc to lead me through the healing work that would forever change my life that evening.

I actually had fun playing along with Coach Marc's request to create a seven-step blueprint called Happiness Anonymous that explained how to renounce happiness and become the most depressed person possible. The brilliance in this exercise was that it forced me to own what I'd been doing to keep myself stuck in depression.

Then I flipped that blueprint to create what I now call my Whole-Person Well-Being blueprint as follows:

1. Accept and learn from your past experiences and move on rather than staying stuck in the pain of the past.

2. Instead of hating yourself, love yourself.

3. Continually feed truth, affirmations, and positive thoughts into your life instead of regularly repeating lots of lies to yourself.

4. Regularly take time to vision new beginnings, possibilities, dreams, and opportunities (instead of sprinkling in thoughts of suicide and despair).

5. Surround yourself with positive, abundance-minded people rather than those stuck in negativity and a scarcity mindset.

6. Take care of yourself. Listen to your body.

7. Quit buying into the medication cocktail solution.

I realized I'd been living with one foot in each blueprint, frequently sabotaging what I knew I needed to do for Whole-Person Well-Being by practicing the Happiness Anonymous plan instead. Seeing these two plans side-by-side, both of which I had created, caused me to realize how I was keeping myself stuck and miserable.

Excavating the Layers

That exercise would have been a substantial breakthrough in itself, but what followed allowed for my full healing and freedom from all the emotional baggage I'd been carrying.

For this exercise I invited people from my past to "sit" in the empty chair opposite me so I could roleplay having a conversation with them. Nuances of long-buried memories rushed to the surface and were released one by one.

First was Ted, the truck driver who spent weekends in my parents' spare bedroom from the time I was two until I was three-and-a-half. Except he didn't stay in his room. What he called "our special time together" was anything but special, and stole my innocence. At the age of three, my imposter-self took over and built walls around my scarred little soul, protecting me, but also preventing me from soaring.

Until four years ago, nightmares about rape had been the only hints of the memories that had been repressed for over thirty years. The afternoon they flooded into my consciousness, God supplied good friends to get me through the awful first forty-eight hours. A therapist skillful in eye movement desensitization and reprocessing (EMDR) helped me continue this healing process over the coming months, allowing me to be no longer bound by the trauma.

I needed to have one last conversation as Ted figuratively sat in the chair opposite me – I forgave him and released him from my heart's prison.

The next person to sit in the chair was an innocent, like me. There had been a naive and harmless exploration one day during preschool naptime when Steve and I compared boy's and girl's parts under the blanket. That should have been a silly, forgotten memory except that I had dumped all of the shame surrounding Ted's violation onto this one incident.

Similarly, I had mislabeled the guilt from cheating on a spelling test as deep shame. Guilt kept me honest. Shame told me I was innately broken and not able to be fixed or accepted. If I was so worthless, my message must be, too! I'd been stuck believing that since I'd been a "bad" person I didn't deserve true happiness, abundance, and success.

Finally, I allowed the light of truth to shine on the dark, core belief that I was inadequate and worthless... that I couldn't receive God's healing and be whole. The eagle may not have died, but it had been chained in that protective cage long enough! It was time to step into my own personal power and deliver my message of help and hope.

After I had sat with each of the other people on my list, I invited my imposter-self to sit in the chair opposite me. As she did, my body contracted into the tightest of fetal positions. I painfully acknowledged her hard work to protect me behind the walls, but told her I no longer needed her and to get lost for good.

In the past, my authentic self could only peek out at the world when I dared to dabble in Whole-Person Well-Being, but my imposter-self would always scream for attention, and I'd quickly run back to the Happiness Anonymous blueprint. I barely knew my authentic self existed.

Coach Marc said that my authentic self requested an invitation to sit by me. She also requested that she be allowed to stay, unlike every other person in the chair I had dismissed and released. I agreed, and as I looked my newly freed authentic self in the mirror, my shoulders and head lifted. I was able to look her in the eyes... with love.

While utterly exhausted from the intense soul-clearing work I'd done, I felt absolutely amazing and freed. The next day everyone around me noticed a significant shift. I was more vibrant, more confident.

Two evenings later, at the close of the event, my next Divine Appointment took the form of a network spinal analysis treatment. My body began a physical unwinding process over two weeks that started with the painful knot in my low back.

The years of pent-up emotion had caused so much joint pain that even getting up from a chair was painful by my mid-thirties. So for me to make a video of myself dancing a tribute to stepping into my authentic, abundant, and powerful self was a testament to the healing I had experienced. Being able to post it on Facebook was even more profound, as I would never have considered sharing my dance with the world previously. Now I'm planning to use dance in my upcoming retreats as a visual portrayal of my powerful healing journey — spiritually, emotionally, and physically.

Striking a New Balance

Stepping into my Whole-Person Well-Being blueprint has helped me learn a new balance in my life. I'd like to share with you some of the steps I've taken to improve my overall health and well-being... in hopes they help you, too.

First off, I've accepted and learned from past hurts, but refuse to allow myself to be chained by them. I also have accepted that I am part of the 20 percent of the population that is highly sensitive. Given my early childhood trauma, this has made me more prone to depression and anxiety, so it is even more important for me to be intentional about how I use my time and the inputs I allow into my life.

I've become fully committed to the journey of learning what it means to love myself and allow my authentic, abundant, and powerful self to soar. I recognize it will likely be a long-term process, as my authentic self has spent nearly forty years with clipped wings. But it begins as I begin to flap my wings and take action.

Resuming my daily habit of reading my Bible continually feeds truth into my life. I try to look for the good in each situation I encounter. When old habits of negative thinking creep in, I consciously turn those thoughts around into a more positive way of talking to myself. I actively seek to be used in the Divine Appointments God places in my path.

107

I keep my long-term vision of my goals for the future in front of me on a weekly basis. I make sure that my action plan for the week is moving me closer to those goals. Practicing accountability with regular support from my coaches keeps me on track.

I've also learned how to set aside quality time to spend with my closest friends and my husband to nurture those relationships, as well as leaning on my new entrepreneur friends and filling my Facebook feed with their success-oriented, abundance-minded posts.

As a highly sensitive person, it is especially important to listen to my body and take care of myself. I am learning to listen to my body's true craving for healthier food choices and have started to cook at home more. Long walks in nature, water aerobics, and dance are things I build into my daily life, as well as ensuring I get enough sleep. I've realized that I also crave time in nature, sunsets, nature photography, and time in the garden with my two cats. When the seasons shift to winter, I allow my artistic side to play indoors again with my stained glass, mosaics, and jewelry-making.

As I've done these other parts of the blueprint, I've been able to wean myself almost entirely off depression and sleep meds, and I need far less pain medication than I have in the past.

In addition to following my own Whole-Person Well-Being blueprint, I am learning to delegate more tasks in my business to allow me to function in my true giftedness rather than just working harder to get it all done. I am more strategic in my business choices as well, including targeting areas of the country where I have a base of existing clients in order to lead three-day retreats.

Now that I've let go of my imposter-self and the walls she built, I can stand in my value as I step into my authentic, abundant, and powerful self. I can proclaim the message of freedom from the silence and the shame around sexual abuse, depression, and anxiety. I can break generational chains of failure and shame around dyslexia and other learning disabilities.

And my hope is that you are inspired and empowered to stand and proclaim whatever it is you need for yourself. I know it sounds cliché, but if I can do this, I know you can, too.

This eagle is soaring!

Beth Ellen Nash founded Wings to Soar Online Academy where dyslexics and other outside-the-box learners gain the skills and confidence to not just survive but thrive in school and in life. Look for her forthcoming books, *Dyslexia Outside-the-Box* and *Thriving as a Highly Sensitive Person*. Consider booking Beth Ellen as a speaker or retreat leader. View Beth Ellen's *Authentic, Abundant, and Powerful Me Tribute* video or schedule a complimentary consultation at www. BethEllenNash.com.

Singing My Song:
Miracles, Music, and Mirth

Lauren Perotti, MA

"I have a dream, a song to sing
To help me cope with anything."
~ Abba

WHENEVER I HEAR DEAN MARTIN CROONING "That's Amore," it conjures up old images — almost like black-and-white Polaroids, of scenes from my Italian family upbringing. Our Italian traditions included weekly gatherings at my grandparents' home to eat, drink, play cards and other games, and sing. All of my cousins, aunts, and uncles, and even great-grandparents, would be there. I can picture my uncle playing his accordion while my dad and others sang along, my grandma making sauce and meatballs in the steamy kitchen, and a house full of laughter, music, smoke, and alcohol, with people cursing and loving, all mixed together into some kind of dramatic sonata.

My family has been a source of many blessings and just as many curses. My trial and my triumph has been to find the miracles within the curses, the light that dispels darkness, and how to make life a symphony by playing my unique part in the orchestra of the universe.

When I was a very young girl, my mother often sang songs with me and to me. She loves to sing, and I didn't learn until many years later that she had never really been encouraged to express this aspect of herself in a significant way, particularly by her mother. Even if she didn't get to be a famous songbird, she was at least able to be a star with me.

We had many music rituals together that I loved and still cherish. My favorite was when she would awaken me in the morning by dancing into my bedroom chirping the red, red robin song written by Harry Wood.

"When the red, red robin comes bob, bob, bobbin' along, along,
There'll be no more sobbin' when he starts throbbin' his old sweet song.
Wake up, wake up you sleepy head,
Get up, get up, get out of bed,
Cheer up, cheer up the sun is red,
Live, love, laugh and be happy..."

Singing was not only a way to express passion, but also a way for all of us to chase away the blues. As the years went by, the harmony was drowned out by the dissonance born of my parents' unrealized dreams and their struggles to raise four young children. When I was seven, my younger sister came along, and then another brother just over a year later. I was really happy to be a big sister and loved to laugh, play, and sing songs with them just as my mother did with me.

But my light of simply being a carefree kid began to dim as our home life became increasingly bleak and chaotic because of my mother's depression, my father's unavailability, angry fighting, and dark secrets that I buried inside me for years – at the expense of my soul. It was as if my mother wanted – silently demanded – that someone take away her burden, and I was handed what felt like an undue responsibility for taking care of the younger ones and the household. I even felt responsible for my Mom's happiness, a responsibility that of course I could never fulfill.

112

I longed to sing the music in my soul and wished the chaos at home would whisk me away on its tornado, away from the gray flatness of my life to some bright, colorful, and happy place over the rainbow. It's not as if I had a dream to become a famous singer as my work in life, but I imagined being in a place where I could ditch my over-responsible role and be my creative self.

Since I was not carried away to this magical place, during my teens I began to pave my own stairway to heaven. I was that girl who had to grow up too quickly, who learned to stuff her emotions and authentic essence under a facade that glittered, who learned how to make everything look like a beautifully wrapped package on the outside and bury what was inside. It felt as if there was a missing part of me that left a dark hole inside, causing me to wonder, "Why am I here?" This feeling stirred in me my lifelong quest to look for the light that could fill that black hole and show me the way to my own Oz.

I often wondered what life was really about, and my spirit was crying to leave. When I was seventeen, I met the guy who would become my husband. We attended college together where we pursued very practical and lucrative career paths — accounting and engineering. Surely achievements, success, and love would be the key to happiness. We moved west, to sunny Southern California, which, at that time, seemed like the Emerald City in the Land of Oz.

Wake Up, Wake Up

As a young woman, my self-identity unconsciously came from other people, places, and things. Soon enough, I was seemingly thriving as a senior manager in an international accounting firm, living in a beautiful Newport Beach townhouse and looking successful... on the outside. I had climbed that corporate ladder quickly and was primed for a promotion to partner in the firm.

I had already gone through the crumbling of my marriage, which cracked open my facade and made me painfully aware again of that black hole inside. This was a blessing, as it sparked my personal development quest. I engaged in psychotherapy; 12-step programs; spiritual and personality assessment systems such as the Myers-Briggs, Enneagram, Numerology, Astrology, Angelology; and more. I uncovered and healed some of those childhood wounds, was working on others, and had begun to get a sense of who I really was and the life I'd love to be living. I was waking up.

With that awakening came my increasing discontent with the deadline-driven demands of my career that kept me focused on meeting and exceeding others' needs and expectations at my own expense. My life was out of balance and I wasn't engaging enough in my passions – singing, the arts, travel, and spirituality. Although there were ways I felt satisfied in that career, there were too many of my talents that were suppressed. I thirsted for something more meaningful, but I felt STUCK. Can you imagine someone who is into the arts, angels and tarot readings sitting in a client's boardroom discussing financial operating results?

Around that time I began to notice that whenever I started to share some of my periodic singing pursuits with my mother, she would change the subject, or worse yet, gush about my musically talented older brother who was also a singer in his own right – and he did want the spotlight and stardom. Somehow it did not threaten her thwarted dream to recognize his musical dream and talent, but she just couldn't do that with me. I could be pretty, smart, and even creative in other ways, but NOT a songbird.

If I shared my emerging dreams with anyone about something more creative I'd really love to pursue as my livelihood, they'd scoff, "You're not going to make any money doing that." It was even more stressful to consider the possibility of starting over in a whole new, but more satisfying career. Just as the French revolutionaries sing in *Les Miserables*, I, too, felt stuck behind a barricade and lost in the valley of the night.

So what happened? My body failed — and bailed me out. I started feeling run down, but convinced myself I was working too hard and just needed a break. Pretty quickly my symptoms grew — fevers and night sweats, lightheadedness to the point of nearly fainting, and unexplained bruises. Clearly something was wrong, but I still kept going.

While at an out-of-town conference, I happened to brush my leg against a table, which immediately brought up a huge hard and black bruise. Now I was scared. When I got back to my hotel room that evening, I stared in the mirror at my pale face and bruised body and couldn't ignore this any longer. I took myself to the emergency room, where I was shockingly diagnosed with acute leukemia.

Leukemia suppresses the normal expression of blood cells. The curse of not being allowed to express and own my creative, musical self, the curse of being made responsible to fulfill another's purpose — this curse that had been passed down the bloodline from grandmother to mother to daughter, had suppressed my soul and my song.

My dis-ease had seeped down to the very core of my bone marrow and was surging through my blood!

It was then that I knew, deep down in the core of my bones, that my survival depended on loving myself enough to fully forgive and release past hurts, claim my life purpose, and live my passion. This deep release freed me to feel immense compassion and love for my mother, who I realized longed to sing her own song. It wasn't until years later that I really understood that my mother had given me an invaluable gift — she had nourished the song in my soul after all.

I did not want to die with my song, my purpose, still in me before I could fully express it! This resolve, and the blessing of the pioneering, passionate blood of my Italian ancestry, activated the resurrecting power in me.

115

I spent the better part of that year in hospitalized isolation, connected 24/7 to a surgically implanted catheter in my chest, being infused with volumes of nuclear-level chemo, blood, antibiotics, and more that I needed for my treatment and to sustain my life! I could not leave the room or detach from the IV pole.

So I transformed what could have been a sterile hospital room into a studio for life-giving creativity: music, singing, movies, and art. After the initial shock of the diagnosis, instead of feeling stuck I was paradoxically freer and more joyful than I had ever been. I laughed and sang from the core of my being, and I claimed my truth – that I am a creative, passionate light worker who also happens to have savvy business and finance acumen. I can and do work with both of these seemingly different aspects of my whole self.

The Talmud, a sacred ancient text of Rabbinic Judaism, says that "Every blade of grass has its angel that bends over it and whispers, 'Grow, grow.'" During that year, Archangels Raphael and Gabriel and so many earth angels surrounded and showered me with powerful waves of healing love. The waves came from family, friends, neighbors, owners of businesses I patronized, my fabulous team of doctors, and even business colleagues from the very firm I had been trying so hard to leave! The more I absorbed the love, the more my life-force energy was able to vibrate at a higher level. I was healed, and my doctors truly considered this a miracle.

Get Up, Get Up

Now I was ready to live the life I envisioned and step confidently in the direction of my dreams. All I needed to do was try! Once I did so, all sorts of things began to occur that never otherwise would have, just as Thoreau discovered in his life experiment about which he wrote in his book *Walden; or Life in the Woods*. After I boldly sold everything I owned and moved to the San Francisco Bay Area, I serendipitously discovered a graduate program that combined my passions. I received

116

a master's degree in psychology and expressive arts therapy that blended theories of psychology, phenomenology, philosophy, the arts, and spirituality.

I was also led to study Life Mastery programs with Mary Morrissey and became certified as a DreamBuilder Coach, which applies the art and science of success and the laws of the universe. Not only that, I studied Life Purpose Hand Analysis, which combines the art of palmistry with the science of fingerprints to decode your soul's blueprint in your hands.

More important, I finally began to blend all of this combined wisdom together into transformational programs and coaching to guide other professionals who feel disconnected from their fire inside, and to shepherd really anyone who desires more aliveness and purpose.

It doesn't really matter what it is you or I are here to do; it's essential for us to get out of bed and take action steps toward the goal. Now I am able to enjoy the journey along the way, especially when I maintain consistent habits that cultivate presence and joy.

Cheer Up, Cheer Up

In addition to music and the arts, there are many purposeful practices that can help you feel happy. One powerful tool I've learned is to actively nurture an attitude of gratitude. When I look for the blessings in my life or situations, everything looks much brighter and I actually feel better. It's not always easy, but it really is simple.

There's so much research that has proven the power of gratitude as a life-enhancing energy. Gratitude is a feeling that results when good things happen, but it can also be intentionally invoked by activities such as keeping a gratitude journal, spending time in nature, and even thinking about someone or something that you really appreciate. Apparently feelings of awe and wonder activate the same part of the brain that produces chemicals for feeling good, namely dopamine and serotonin.

Most important, people who have a sense of purpose for their lives or who have identified goals have been found to feel more hopeful and satisfied, even in the face of trials. I am grateful to have discovered my divine destiny and the life goals that align with it, and for having the tools to guide others to do the same.

Live, Love, Laugh

Life to me is like a piece of music. When all of the elements are balanced, it's a harmonious symphony.

Today I am an advocate for living your passion. I live my own life traveling near and far with my life partner, laughing, singing, and skipping along my personal Yellow Brick Road.

"What if I've been blue, now I'm walking through
fields of flowers,
Rain may glisten but still I listen for hours and hours.
I'm just a kid again, doing what I did again, singing a song,
When the red, red robin comes bob, bob, bobbin' along..."

Along the way I lead others I meet to discover that while travelling to Oz, what you are looking for is already within you. You are a spark of the Divine, and you, too, take part in the mighty orchestra of the universe.

Lauren Perotti is a transformational speaker, author, and coach who guides spiritual seekers whose success rings hollow to ignite the fire of their purpose, passion, and power. Blending over thirty years of expertise in business, psychology and the arts, Lauren's creative programs give you tools to align your life with your highest vision and make your life a masterpiece. Visit www.LaurenPerotti.com to claim her gift and kickstart your journey to be energized, empowered, and enlightened.

The Time Is Now –
Are You Ready?

Lilia Shoshanna Rae

I LOOKED OUT INTO THE FACES of 500 light workers gathered to celebrate our reunion in the crystal vortex of Hot Springs, Arkansas. My friend Linda and I stood on the stage holding wooden staffs representing the energy of the Divine Feminine and Divine Masculine, jointly delivering messages for each of us to embody the gifts of both. We were leading the opening ceremony for the final segment of a three-day experience for this group. All of us had listened to many speakers who regularly deliver their messages to thousands through TV, YouTube, and more. The originator of the conference was set to deliver his message from Spirit as the highlight of the event. Here we were. It was our turn. Were we ready?

Linda delivered her message from the Divine Feminine. It was one she had received in the Queen's Chamber of the Great Pyramid. (She describes the message in her story which is next in this book.) Now it was my turn to deliver the message from the Divine Masculine. This message had come to me as we planned the presentation the day before, setting the intent to deliver what was needed for this group in this moment that was being so divinely orchestrated.

I took a strong stance on the stage, allowing the energy flowing through the staff to support me and keep me fully aligned with the Divine. I spoke, sharing the following message that came through me from the great Egyptian god, Thoth:

Be who you came to be in these bodies.
Do what you came to do in these bodies.
Those in Spirit cannot do what you can do in your bodies.
The time is now.

Linda then led everyone in a meditation of setting intentions for what each would do when leaving the event. I led the group in a chant to seal the energy of the intentions. It was done. We had answered the call and spoken our truth.

Later I asked myself, who was really speaking on that stage? Was it me? Or was it really Thoth through me? Did it even matter? The message itself was important. What I know is in that moment, I stood tall, spoke with courage and conviction, felt waves of energy flow through me as they only do when I feel I speak my truth, and the message was not one that would normally come out of my mouth.

For me, this was a graduation ceremony of sorts. For years I had been hearing messages from the angelic realm. The messages started with my guardian angel coming in to sooth my broken heart. Not long after, Archangel Michael began comforting me and reminding me of some basic truths of all existence. That I am lovable. I am loved. I am love.

Soon after these encounters, I began to hear from others: Saint Germain, Melchizedek, Jesus, Mary, and many more. These communications were not something I learned from books or teachers, although I turned to both to confirm I was not crazy. The messages came through meditation and contemplation. I was searching for the meaning of life — my life and all life. Who does not do that at least at some point while living in a human body? If we do not come to this focus of contemplation naturally, a life crisis usually throws us onto our knees and has us implore, "What is this life thing all about? Why am I suffering? Why do I not feel love? Why am I even living? What is the purpose? What is my purpose? Who am I? Who is God? Is there really something that is God?"

Most of my life crises have centered on aspects of love: Not feeling loved. Not loving someone who wanted to be loved. Not loving myself. Being threatened with serious physical harm by a husband who said he loved me, but nearly killed me the last time we "made love." Betrayal by the next two loves, the second of whom I was sure was my soul mate destined to be my ultimate partner for this lifetime, only to find out that he chose my best friend for an interlude instead. And lastly, not finding any love better than the one I left behind before getting married.

In the spaciousness of the hole in my heart, where lost love broke it wide open, came the messages of light and truth reminding me that true love is something much greater than what we worship or idealize as human love. As I recorded these messages over the years, I told few about them. I did not fully trust that what was coming through me was coming through those I identified as the senders. What if I was making it up? What if I was actually delusional and these were mere constructs of my imagination resulting from my despair and brokenness? How could I distinguish what was true from what was illusion?

Instead, I chose to keep the messages private. Close friends knew of them, and a few actually read them or witnessed my receiving them. Occasionally I would speak them during healing sessions I gave as a Reiki master. After fifteen years of receiving these messages, I now feel confident they are true – or at least as true as I, as a human, can convey them. Our bodies, after all, are creations in the material world. Distortion of truth exists in this three-dimensional realm of duality. It is only through deep discernment and practice that one can connect clearly with the truths in the spiritual realms. Even the clearest channels of spiritual wisdom have some level of distortion in their messages. It could not be otherwise when they speak in words, for words can only approximate truth. Those who have experienced a *samadhi* or ecstatic state of blissfulness, or who have returned from a near-death experience, say they cannot express the full extent of the experience. These types of experiences are "ineffable" or indescribable in language known to humankind.

I now can no longer keep these messages to myself. The world needs to hear from these beings of light and love. Even more, each of us needs to open up to messages from the Divine as fully as possible. Whether the messages come through prayer and are perceived to come directly from God or Jesus or come through angels or other enlightened beings, we are each receptors of divine wisdom. We need only clear ourselves of human blocks.

How do we become the clear vessels of divine wisdom? It is easier said than accomplished. It is an ongoing process. Discernment of truth occurs in each moment. There is no place called Truth while in human form. It may exist in spiritual realms, but while we are in human bodies the distortion of the material world must be addressed moment to moment.

Does this process have to be so serious? I tend to make it so and then laugh at myself for forgetting to "lighten" up. If I am not feeling joy along with truth and love, I realize I have missed an essential piece of my journey. I take a step back and observe myself to see whether I am feeling happiness in the mix of my spiritual practice. If not, I recognize that some old belief is keeping me from the natural state of bliss.

I like to think back to when I was a child. I did not have a perfect childhood (my parents argued, we did not have much money, my mother was very strict, and people called me "Carrot Top" because of my red hair). I know now I was blessed in many other ways. I had gifts as a child that only now I am claiming for myself as an adult. Courage is one of them. Picture a little five-year-old girl with flaming red hair — an almost orange red that fades as a redhead grows older but that compels well-meaning adults to humiliate her by using the reference to a carrot or rubbing her hair for good luck. Then see her in green tights, a green tunic, and a cap like the one worn by Robin Hood. Imagine her standing in the middle of a stage in a play before an audience filled with expectant, anxious parents, holding a wooden sword up high, loudly proclaiming, "I am Pigwiggen, the Brave, and I stand here for what is right!"

I smile to this day in remembering that moment. Where in the world did I find such courage when I was so young? How did I lose it as an adult? How did I lose the sense of playfulness and passion? I was definitely delivering a message back then, even if it was not my own. I delivered it with confidence and conviction that I want to emulate as an adult, yet it was part of a children's play. By remembering this precious moment of childlike innocent courage, I can bring more of that quality into the present moment.

I could have used some of that courage during my marriage. Instead, I gave away so much of what was important to me — friendships, fun, and freedom — to keep the peace between my husband and me. I was deeply afraid that if I stood up for myself I would be harmed. I was so scared that I often found myself crouching down in the corner of our dining room because I wanted some sense of protection, even if only from two walls. I felt fear, despair, and no hope. When I spoke up I was accused of crazy infidelity. After all, I had said hello to the man who lived across the street from us. I had been five minutes late from work. What had I been doing? Who was I with? What about the men at work? Was I sleeping with them?

These were the types of questions I was asked for hours on end each day for six months. When the questions turned to accusations, threats followed. I knew I had to do something, but what? I was afraid that if I did anything — ran away, spoke back to him, or stood up for myself — something worse would happen. I felt powerless. This

125

angry, possessed man had resources and abilities against which I was defenseless. He was sure to find me if I left with our two kids. The fact that I was pregnant with his third did not quiet his interrogations and menacing allegations. What would he be like if I left?

Somehow, with the help of my parents (who had no clue what was going on before I called them in desperation), I found the courage to leave and never return to the marriage. Through the grace of God the threats turned to pleas. The monster turned meek and mild, begging me to return. Having learned after leaving that the new behavior was merely a predictable part of the cycle of abusive relationships, I refused. My psychotherapist and parents supported me in this healthy decision. He finally left the area and our lives forever. In some ways I felt bad that my children no longer had their father in their life, but deep down I knew they would never have the peace we experienced if he were around.

That was the lowest point in my life — cowering in the corner of my dining room, having no hope, consumed with fear. A friend who witnessed how I was then and how I am now has given me a beautiful image. She says I have been like a little flower growing, despite all odds, in a crack in the sidewalk, who is now standing tall and strong like a huge sunflower — even standing tall in front of hundreds at a conference of light workers sharing Thoth's message.

There is so much more to life. As Thoth reminds us, those in Spirit cannot do what we can do in these bodies. The principle of free will for humankind prevents their taking action in our realm without permission. Each of us is here for a reason. Our lives have meaning. Your life has meaning. Do you know what it is?

I know that as part of my purpose I am to embody as much love and light as I can and be a clear vessel for messages from Spirit. My five-year-old self is teaching me to deliver it with courage, confidence, and conviction. My adult self is listening, clearing blocks, and standing up on stage asking me and you, "How can you be who you came into this life to be? How can you do what you came to do?"

The time is now. Are you ready?

Lilia Shoshanna Rae's mission is to help clients live Heaven on Earth, attaining deep peace and joy through meditation and healing practices. During Reiki sessions, she delivers messages from angels and accesses star energy to give clients new perspective on their soul's purpose. She loves to teach classes on the sacred mysteries of alchemy, sacred geometry, and the Enneagram to help clients transform and transcend. Find her blog and a sample meditation at LiliaShoshannaRae.com.

Encountering the Mystery

Linda T. Roebuck, MA, Counseling Psychology

"WHY WOULD YOU WANT TO GO TO EGYPT NOW? You know the trouble that's happening over there. We may never see you again. Your ninety-six-year-old mother may not be alive when you return. I could never forgive myself if she were my mother." Such comments were being made by my family and friends. Add to those my own inner critic's voice: "What do you think you are doing? You might become immobilized while entering or exiting the Great Pyramid. What if you freeze up and there's a group of people behind you? What if your body isn't fit enough to handle the trip? Will there be enough air inside the pyramid? Could you forgive yourself if your mother dies while you're away?"

Unreasonable thoughts of fear and guilt ran rampant in my mind. My leaving on this trip didn't make sense to others and it didn't make sense to me. Yet something more powerful than the voices of fear and guilt was pulling me to Egypt in early 2012, and I followed it. It was one of the few times in my life that I didn't care what other people thought or said about me. I felt alive and in some strange way, on purpose.

Before signing up for this trip, I had received a call from our leader. This was to be a pilgrimage, not a tourist event. The leader is a visionary, intuitive, and channel, and is also someone I respect. He shared that this journey would be very healing for me and that I would have an opportunity to remember and transcend past life wounds. Those words resonated with me. At that moment, I decided to trust my overwhelming "inner guidance" with a "Yes, I am in!" I had had visions/dreams/memories of being suffocated in some type of initiation or rite in a pyramid; I was now ready and willing to face my fears.

Our leader also stated that I was a code carrier and that I would know what to do with the code when the time came. I didn't understand. What is a code? How could I be carrying a code and not know it? However, I trusted in positive outcomes and allowed "the how" to show up differently than I had thought it would.

I knew I had made the right decision to go to Egypt because when the plane landed in Cairo on January 28th, 2012, I felt exhilarated and peaceful. Making my way to the hotel by taxi was easy and almost effortless as I relaxed into my decision to be fully present. The next day I met my roommate from England. It was a perfect match. We related on many levels and also gave each other space and privacy. We became tight friends with two other women and spent a lot of time meditating and doing rituals with them. Snake energy seemed to be present everywhere we went. We noticed the cobra (uraeus) on the diadems (crowns) of the different gods and goddesses and started calling ourselves "Ssssisters" as we would hiss and make snakelike gestures with our fingers.

One of the "Ssssisters" has a brother, an Egyptologist, who spends half the year in Luxor, Egypt, and the other half in Chicago, USA. His responsibility is overseeing excavation and research in the Karnak Temple Complex. We were fortunate that he was in the area at the time we were there. Learning that he had made arrangements to take the four of us on a private tour was beyond any expectation I could have thought up. How excited we were when he and his driver picked us up outside of the hotel early one morning to go to the site.

The beautiful and elevating experiences we shared set the tone for my amazing visit to the Temple of Sekhmet located on the Karnak temple site. Sekhmet is a lioness-headed goddess whose image can be found all over Egypt. In every site we visited, I looked for her image in statue, carving, and painting. Sekhmet's name is derived from the ancient Egyptian word *sekhem,* which stands for power or might. Her name suits her purpose as it conveys the one who is powerful.

On the first day in Cairo, I had purchased a small carving of Sekhmet's head made out of lapis lazuli which I was told was the "real deal." I kept it near me during the whole journey. My friend's brother verified that the artifact I was carrying was indeed very ancient. It does possess an unusual and special energy. I hold it when I want to get centered and open to receiving messages from my heart.

Sekhmet's temple had been closed and we were not sure it would be accessible while we were there. Letting go of expectation, we were delighted to discover that it would be open for a short time that day. I didn't take many photos during the entire trip; however, I did take a picture with my phone in Sekhmet's temple. The existence of numerous orbs that showed up in the photo affirmed the palpable feeling of energy I experienced. Little did I know that this was leading me to a profound message from the Goddess.

The next day we boarded a cruise ship that would take us up the Nile and back to Cairo. Being on this famous river for the first time was exhilarating and I was mesmerized and moved as the giant ship passed unforgettable scenes of beauty. While in meditation and looking at the river, I asked the Universe about my code. A very clear message came: "You carry your code in your body, in your spine." "Interesting," I thought. "I still don't have a clue about what it is or what to do with it."

On the Nile I experienced even more insights than I ever expected. Another member of our group had also connected with the Sekhmet energy and told our leader about it. Our leader told the two of us that we should talk about our shared experience. The opportunity to chat occurred the next day on the top deck of our cruise ship. It was one of those synchronistic moments, witnessed by our friends as well as the two of us, when deep memories of a past life flooded through me. I recalled a time when I had initiated or ordained priests or priestesses. As I shared my remembrance, a holy moment occurred. I knew this was the time to share the lapis lazuli pendant I had intuitively brought with me on this pilgrimage. A deep knowing came over me. The intention, words, and gestures were almost automatic. I was in such an altered state during this period that I don't recall what I said, but the love and intention brought tears to all our eyes.

From this experience I began gaining a sense and feeling of Who I Am. The old tape that had played in my head so often, "Who do you think you are?" was now much softer. It was being replaced by the Truth of who I really am. I am Love expressing as Linda.

Our pilgrimage culminated with a visit to the Great Pyramid in Giza. The pyramid would be open only for our group and we would have two hours of visitation time. The excitement started building as we waited in silence to enter. I focused on being present and taking each step consciously. We ascended to the King's Chamber and found a place to sit around the sides of the room. We began chanting and taking turns getting into the sarcophagus, helping each other in and out as the energy built. Vibrations, visions, memories, and knowing filled the area. As the frequency increased, we received word that they were going to open the Queen's Chamber for our group. The Queen's Chamber had been closed for a long time so this was a delightful surprise, even though fear began to show up in me.

As we descended the narrow corridor to the Queen's Chamber, I had an overwhelming sense that this was the place where I was to release my code. I found a spot to sit with my back leaning against the wall of the chamber. I began to meditate with the intention to release the code that I carried in my spine. I can't explain the energy that was surging through my being. While I was in this state, our leader called me to come to the center of the room and asked me to give a message from Sekhmet. It was unexpected and I felt that I could not say no to the request. So I slowly moved to the center of the room, knelt on my knees, took a deep breath, and opened my mouth. All of a sudden a voice came through me and started speaking in a language I did not know. The voice was not my voice. I knew the message was for me, but as I looked around I also knew it was targeted to many others in the chamber.

We were in reflective silence as we exited the pyramid and boarded the bus. I took out my journal so I could remember the messages that came through me from Sekhmet. The four themes are:

Step into your power; the power is Love!
Quit playing small!
Love yourself, *fiercely!*
Protect that which is sacred — your own Sacred Heart!

They are as profound for me today as they were when they were revealed. If you resonate to these messages, then there is a good chance you are being called to truly love who you are, to stand up for your truth, to claim your power in a situation or relationship, and to guard against forces that would harm or diminish Love in the world.

Cameras were not allowed in the pyramid; however, a few of our group took some pictures. There is an alcove in the Queen's Chamber where several of us were standing to get photographed. In a photo that my friend took, a clear image of an energetic golden snake appeared. I was blown away. The snake was shaped like my spine. I have scoliosis, and the curve in the snake replicated the curve in my spine. Confirmation that mission was accomplished? Yes!

An encounter with the "mystery" is really an encounter with "my-story." What a revelation! And, it continues.

I had been changed, and I knew I had been a channel for others to experience transformation. As I was meditating in my family room a couple of days after returning home, I heard the words "Open your eyes." Something caught my attention and I was shocked to see a four-and-a-half-foot-long black snake crawling over crystals on a small table about three feet from me. I stayed very still and watched as it moved from the table to the fireplace, and disappeared. Still in disbelief since this was the cold month of February and snakes were supposed to be in hibernation, I conveyed the event to my husband. He was amused, but didn't try to make sense out of it.

About four months later, he was grilling outside and noticed something on a nearby shrub. As he inspected it, he discovered a fully intact snake skin — four-and-a-half feet long. He brought it inside for me to see and I instantly knew that was the snake I had encountered in the winter. We were quite taken by this remarkable gift and took several pictures of it. Grateful that it was no longer in the house, I opened myself to the messages it brought. According to Ted Andrews in *Animal Speak,* snakes represent rebirth, resurrection, initiation, and wisdom. I identified with each one of those characteristics which had been associated with Snake Medicine while on the pilgrimage. Now it is my gift and opportunity to pass them on to others by sharing my experience.

As an end note, my mother waited not only until I got home from Egypt to make her transition, but until she could *see* that I was home. I had the honor of being by her side as she took her last breath on February 25th, 2012. Now, more than ever, I understand what it means to boldly go into the unknown where I have never dared to go before. As I set the intention to stay open and fully present, I can choose to follow inner guidance and consciously participate in The Great Mystery.

Linda T. Roebuck founded A Community of Transformation (ACT), a non-profit educational organization, in 2001, whose focus is on holistic health: www.ActAnnapolis.org. A teaching Usui and Karuna Reiki® Master, Linda is a gifted spiritual mentor, catalyst for change, and facilitator of remembering ancient knowledge. Her business, Linda Roebuck and Associates, LLC, offers programs, training, and individual sessions using the Alchemical Attunement and Activation (AAA) Healing© system she developed. Her website is www.LindaRoebuck.com.

It's Not Luck – It's a Choice

Christine Rosas

"IF I'D MET YOU BACK THEN, would you have treated me any differently?" I asked my therapist during a recent phone call. "When I first met you, I was pretty much a mess. I was even more of a mess back when I was a teenager. Maybe the opinions of professionals that led me to believe I needed to live a life of limitations were valid."

"No. I wouldn't have treated you differently. I would have gone about things the same way I did," my therapist responded.

"Thank you. That means a lot to me," I graciously expressed to him.

I didn't always believe my current therapist could see past my symptoms to help me. When I first met him in my late twenties, he explained to me that I could be the person I was always meant to be and live the life of my dreams. And he enthusiastically exclaimed that he was going to help me get there.

I thought he was crazy.

In the fifteen-plus years of explaining my story to doctors, psychiatrists, psychologists, and therapists, I don't recall anyone announcing such promises. Sure, they all helped me on some level to get out of challenging situations and into a life that felt more enjoyable, but never to a level that I could celebrate as a complete dream come true. I had given up on that possibility years before.

Yet there I was agreeing to revisit cognitive therapy techniques (didn't quite help me the first time around) and to try group therapy (always saw that as a bunch of whiners in a circle), although I did so half-heartedly. I had to play it safe. I couldn't allow myself to feel too much hope. I usually walked away with a heart full of broken, never-fulfilled dreams. These situations typically started out promising, but always ended with a "There's not much more I can do for you."

Searching for answers began in my teenage years. The opinions of doctors and other professionals led me to conclude that I had to live a life of choices based on limitations due to a diagnosis of clinical depression. For me this meant they believed I couldn't handle going away to college. If I wanted to go to college while staying at home, I most likely couldn't work while doing so. I could handle a job after college, possibly marriage, although if I wanted to have children I'd have to choose between a career and motherhood. Anytime I became overwhelmed and stressed, I was to use those feelings as a warning sign that I wasn't able to handle the life I had created. If I didn't take care in recognizing exhaustion, irritability, or brain fog as a sign I was taking on too much, I usually fell into a deep depressive episode. This was the definitive sign that my choices were not compatible with my limitations. I would have to reevaluate my life to see what I needed to give up.

By my early twenties I was convinced this life of limitations made sense. My life at that point seemed to be proof that I couldn't choose to have it all. Although I finished college, found a job, and decided to move out on my own, I couldn't seem to lead a fulfilling life. It was challenging to keep my apartment clean. I showed up late to almost any commitment I made. I was unhappy with my career and relationship choices. Making decisions became so difficult that I became literally paralyzed by fear.

I began exhibiting physical symptoms similar to MS or a stroke. Natural/holistic practitioners felt something was medically wrong. Neurologists said it was psychosomatic and I had to reduce the stress in my life. So I attempted to become even more practical and cautious. A part of me craved adventure, but my attempts to live more carefree and adventurously usually ended in poor choices. I realized I simply had to come to terms with the fact that I wasn't wired to have it all.

As the years went by, my inner struggle continued. A part of me was fearful of following my instincts, while another part of me knew that if I could just step out of the fear, my true self would shine through. And there were moments when I did just that. I became a freelance graphic designer, got married, and had a daughter. Something still seemed like it wasn't quite right. Any time my stress level rose, I again felt emotionally and physically paralyzed by fear.

Thankfully this happened around the time I met my current therapist. Even through all my initial apprehensions, he saw past my symptoms to a part of me that was fully capable of living a fulfilled life. I worked with him to dive deep, past my surface-level issues, and get to the root cause of my challenges.

I began to realize that I saw overwhelm and stress as signs that I was incapable of making proper choices. This caused me to withdraw and never express my true self. I learned that when I became angry, I turned that anger inward even if the dilemma was not my fault. My therapist explained that these were signs of situational depression, not clinical depression. It wasn't life itself that I was incapable of handling; it was my *perception* of my life that created inner conflict and challenges.

Because of the negative belief system I adopted in my adolescence, I became over-cautious and second-guessed my adventurous spirit. However, my spirit was so strong that it was hard to ignore it. I'm thankful it never stopped screaming for my attention, and even more thankful that I chose to learn how to listen to it.

As I learned new ways to process and express challenging emotions, I found myself handling everyday life with greater ease. I didn't take people's actions so personally. I didn't give in to unnecessary drama. It all began with figuring out who I truly was and listening to my true self.

This led to one of the biggest adventures of my life: moving from the US to Australia. Visiting Australia had been a dream of mine since I had been five years old. I grew up in the northeastern part of the US, and recall my kindergarten friends saying they wanted to visit Florida, even Hawaii. Nope, not me. I wanted to go farther. So when my husband received a job offer in Australia, I knew we had to go.

On paper, moving to Australia did not look like a good option, because the opportunity arose during the financial crisis of 2008. Just as my husband signed his contract, the Australian dollar took a nosedive. This meant we had lost twenty percent of what we needed to meet our current US bills. We owed more on our house than it was worth and had other major debt to pay off. However, through it all, my heart knew we were meant to go.

So, for the first time in my life, I listened to my heart and didn't act out in fear. When my black-and-white-thinking civil-engineer husband asked me to give him one good reason why we should uproot ourselves and our three-and-a-half-year-old daughter and move halfway around the world at a time like this, I responded, "Because I want to." Of course he found this ridiculous, but I continued to push. And off we went.

It turned out to be one of the best decisions of our lives. The Australian dollar became stronger and our savings grew. We paid off debt, found renters for our US home, and kept up with our mortgage payments. We grew stronger as a couple and as individuals. We learned that home is where the heart is and that it isn't based on material items or location. We learned that we can live simpler yet more fulfilling lives. My husband's work experience took him to career levels that would have taken him three times as long to reach if we had stayed in the US. Best of all, our family grew by one more member. I gave birth to our son in Australia.

Some believe I was lucky to find the therapist I had found. Others believe I am even luckier to have the time and financial means to commit to inner exploration. But I don't see it as luck. I see it as a choice. I chose to do the work. I chose to commit time, energy, and resources to becoming the person I was meant to be. I dug deep and gained the courage to silence the inner and outer critics in order to listen to my true wants and needs. And I continue to do so each day.

I'm constantly challenged by my apprehension to accept change and uncertainty. I can't stand "going with the flow." My adventurous spirit continues to be trapped in a control freak's body. However, I have allowed my spirit more time to play. Sometimes it means becoming more creative in my parenting style with my kids. Other times it means taking larger adventurous leaps and traveling more often as a family. My ten-year-old daughter has traveled to nineteen countries, and my five-year-old son to seventeen!

My life experiences have also helped me redefine the role that fear plays in my life. I no longer see fear as something that needs to be conquered or overcome. I see fear as a friend getting my attention to pause for a moment to see if I really want to head in the direction I'm going.

I have also gained the ability to fully trust my instincts and listen to my heart-centered desires. When my emotions get the best of me, I am able to admit that I need to take a break.

All these experiences brought me to where I am today. At the time of writing this chapter, we are living in Saudi Arabia. We chose to move because of my husband's inner feeling that Australia was no longer fulfilling all parts of him. However, after living here for one year, we have decided that it's in the best interest of our family for our kids and me to move to the US. My husband will continue to work in Saudi Arabia and visit us about every eight weeks.

This decision has brought with it a tremendous amount of mixed emotions. I have had to dive deep into discomfort and leap further out of my comfort zone than I ever have. My success in sticking with the facts and not adding any unnecessary drama is a daily choice.

Many times my old belief system wishes to creep in and cause havoc in all the progress I've made. Our life has now become quite unconventional compared to the world in which I grew up. The choices require me to completely go within and listen to my heart.

Although I have had some larger-than-life experiences, I don't believe there was one definitive moment that led me to make changes in my life. There also hasn't been a magic pill or one systematic process that allows me to feel as though I'm living as my true self. I believe living the life of my dreams means that I take life one step at a time. I accept what's right in front of me. I recognize when attitudes and perspectives no longer serve me and make an adjustment. I tell my inner control freak "Thanks, but no thanks" more times than not. I allow my adventurous spirit to lead the way to the best experiences of my life.

Although Christine Rosas has lived on three continents, traveled to twenty-three countries, and covered thirteen thousand miles in eighty-three days on a US road trip with her kids in a mini-van, she doesn't consider herself an adventurer. Christine is simply someone who believes in the power of living outside your comfort zone. Download her free ebook, *How to Face Your Fears and Embrace Your True Self,* at www.ChristineRosas.com.

Riding the Dragon: A Journey into the Sacred Purpose of Cancer

Alistair Smith

A Personal Odyssey

IN JANUARY OF 2013, I was diagnosed with stage four cancer. The medical specialists told me that it was terminal and that the average life expectancy was two years. In that moment I was faced with a decision. I could accept the prevailing belief that cancer is a deadly disease and once it reaches a certain stage cannot be reversed. Alternatively, I could see this as an invitation from Life, which I have come to see as an intelligent, primal force, to engage in a deeper relationship with her: one that would bring me back into harmony with the natural state of creation.

I chose the second option and embarked on a journey that would reveal great mysteries that I'd only been able to intellectually glimpse before.

Perhaps the most important thing that emerged from this journey is how integrated our universe is. It's like a fractal with the same energy playing out at every level of existence. What this means is that the cancer playing out its potentially deadly dance in my body is manifesting the same energy as the cancerous actions manifesting on the global scene that are leading humanity towards the brink of extinction.

I also uncovered a profound healing capacity that exists at the cellular level of the body, or perhaps even deeper. This is a sacred force aligned to Life that can rise up out of the cellular structure and sweep away disease if that is what is in the best interests of the whole. This emergent phenomenon is what lies at the root of cases of radical remission in which cancer gradually (and sometimes suddenly) disappears from the body against all medical odds.

After diving into the root energy of cancer, I came to see that this disease has a higher purpose in our lives; we might even call it a sacred purpose. It is Life's way of showing us what will happen to the global body of humanity if we continue to live in the way we have been up till now. But not only this, it is also giving us insight into what we need to do in order to change the course of the direction that civilization is taking.

If I am to live through this current challenge, I must change the story of my life, effectively reinventing myself as an incarnate being. That reinvented self will be one who is not acting in pursuit of its own personal glory, but in deeply sacred service to Life. I believe that when I can reach this state of surrender, the healing power within will be activated and sweep forth to bring healing to my body if, and only if, this serves the larger evolutionary purpose.

The same thing can happen at the collective level.

For this healing to take place, however, I must first assume complete responsibility for what I am creating. I need to accept ownership for the cancerous cells in my body and desist from assuming the role of a victim. In the same way, if we are to heal the global body, we must first accept responsibility for what we are jointly creating in the collective space. Only then will the transformational healing that is required to shift the direction of human civilization become possible.

Rebellion against Life

In my journey into the core of cancer, I first sought to understand exactly what a cancer cell is. Every single cell in the body has a sacred covenant with Life under which it plays its part in maintaining the integrity and harmony of the overall system. As part of that covenant, every cell offers itself willingly into the arms of death after a certain period of time, enabling new cells to be born. This enables Life to circulate her loving presence throughout the body, constantly moving her energy through every organ and system.

A cancer cell is one that breaks this sacred covenant. Cancer cells are dangerous because they do not die; they seek immortality within the body. Consequently, when they reproduce, they just keep getting bigger and bigger without the associated death of existing cells.

We can say, therefore, that a cancer cell is one that pursues its own agenda rather than playing the role it was drawn into incarnation to play.

How does this happen? A cancer cell is, after all, just that: a cell within the body. So how can it suddenly become rogue and act in a way that is destructive to the body as a whole? The answer lies in the information that supports cells.

Each organ and system in the body is supported by fields of information that transmit into the cells telling them what role they are meant to play. It is this information that tells a liver cell what aspects of the DNA program to switch on to enable it to function as a liver cell. In a cancer cell, the healthy information field is hijacked and replaced by a new field, one that is intent on imposing its will on Life.

Cancer is an ancient phenomenon. It has been around for about 1.5 billion years. But there is little doubt that this disease is growing alarmingly in modern Western nations. This goes against the trend of reduction of most diseases due to medical breakthroughs, and there is a very good reason for this phenomenon. There are stark parallels between the behavior of a cancer cell and the way we, as modern humans, behave. Indigenous people around the world have always known that they were part of a larger universe and understood how important it was to honor all of life and the environment in which they walked. Like a healthy cell, they understood their role in maintaining harmony in the larger global body. As modern, Western people, we have lost this understanding. Not only have we disconnected from our natural roots, but we have disconnected from our society and often even our families. Each family has become a separate unit driven to accumulate as much money and possessions it feels it needs in order to be secure.

We are, in short, acting like cancer cells. So it is little wonder that cancer is manifesting so powerfully in our lives today as Life uses this phenomenon to show us what we are doing to ourselves.

The World: Stage Four Cancer

Cancer is often depicted as occurring in stages, with stage four being the highest and most serious. Generally stage four cancer, which means the cancer has spread from its original site to another organ, is considered terminal. From the view I have looking at the world from the inside out, our planet moved to a state of stage four cancer in the middle to late 1990s.

When I researched the way cancer spreads throughout the body, I was struck by the remarkable similarity to the way a global corporation moves into a foreign country, enlists the support of local officials and middlemen, and then plunders the resources of that nation, often with little regard for the well-being of the people. It is much the same way that metastatic cancer moves into a new organ and begins to consume the resources of that organ without any regard for the healthy cells.

146

Until 1990 the world was locked in an ideological battle between two titanic forces led by the United States and the Soviet Union. With the fall of the Berlin Wall, this battle came to an end, opening the door for the next step in our planet's collective journey. In the subsequent ten years, dramatic changes were made to the rules governing trade and banking, with virtually every nation opening itself to foreign investment and trade.

Until this time corporations were largely confined to their home countries, but with the end of the Cold War they were able to spread their tentacles across the globe. It does not take a genius to reach the conclusion that our current path on this planet is unsustainable. Even putting aside climate change, the rate at which we are consuming resources is depleting natural stocks of fish, water, and arable land at an alarming rate. The corporate world needs continual growth to feed its incessant hunger, and in order for this growth to be sustained it must continue to open up new markets. With globalization in full swing, the entire world is being sold on the American Dream.

In order for China, India, and the rest of the developing world to reach a certain standard of living, namely the same level of consumption as the US, it will require an increase of about ten times the current resource consumption. Clearly this is unsustainable short of some miraculous new technology that allows us to manufacture everything we need from the ether.

Just like a cancerous tumor that devours the resources of the body at a rate that is unsustainable and eventually leads to death, we have created a society that is devouring the resources of our planet at a rate that cannot be sustained. Unless we change the collective story we are living, there will be no future for humanity.

Chemical Warfare

The Australian medical system has very few options for treating cancer. They basically consist of surgery, chemotherapy, and radiation.

I have had two major surgeries and completed seventy weeks of chemotherapy. I was very resistant to doing chemotherapy, but my inner guidance was that I needed to undergo it, that there were things to learn. So what does chemotherapy represent in the global sphere?

Chemotherapy involves the infusion of toxic chemicals into the body, usually in a systemic way, which means it flows through the entire system. The chemicals are designed to attack any cell that is fast-growing because this is one of the characteristics of cancer cells. At the same time, however, they also attack the fast-growing cells in the mouth, stomach, and bone marrow. In the process they weaken the immune system and place a great burden on the entire body.

Chemotherapy is often effective in the short term, causing a reduction in tumor size, as it did with mine. But cancer is extremely clever and eventually builds immunity against the drugs, which cease to work, and the cancer comes back stronger than ever.

Cancer is a multifaceted phenomenon that displays many different qualities that can also be found in the larger global environment. In many ways cancer is similar to a terrorist organization. Someone who has been diagnosed with cancer lives in constant tension waiting for the next scan or blood test result. They know that the cancer can flow invisibly around the body and suddenly emerge at some distant location without warning. Terrorists behave in a similar manner. A great deal of the fear invoked by terrorists arises from the fact that they inhabit an unseen world and can launch a sudden attack anywhere on the planet.

In this context, chemotherapy in the body is the equivalent of the global war on terror in the global body. The US government launched an official war on cancer many years ago, and it is no surprise that it launched a similar war on terror a few decades later.

We can see that the war on terror has followed exactly the same pathway that chemotherapy does. Initially there is some gain. Some terrorist cells are destroyed and a few senior terrorists are captured or killed. In the process, however, many innocent people are killed (just as healthy cells in the body are destroyed by chemotherapy), and this destruction breaks the fabric of the community under attack and creates a simmering resentment that is ripe for cultivating a whole new generation of terrorists. The destruction to community that occurs when the US and its allies attack a region like Iraq or Afghanistan is very similar to the breakdown in the immune system that occurs in the human body through chemotherapy. In both cases, while there may be short-term gains, it does not offer a viable long-term solution.

The Global Immune System

Cancer survives so well in the body because it has devised very clever means of enlisting the support of the immune system to cloak its presence. Cancer cells actually hijack aspects of the immune system and get it to send messages to the body telling it that these are cells that need to be protected. The main functions of the immune system are to first identify anything that is harmful to the harmonious functioning of the body, and then destroy those harmful elements. What exactly is the immune system and where can we find it in the global sphere?

In a global sense the identification element most closely resembles the media, especially investigative journalists on whom we rely to expose corruption. The judicial system and all the power that sits behind it is then tasked with dealing with those people or organizations who are acting in ways that are harmful to the overall community.

If we consider global corporations to be the collective manifestation of a cancer tumor, devouring the resources of the planet, we can see what a mess our global immune system is in. The mainstream media is owned almost exclusively by the same people who own the global corporations. In other words, cancer owns the immune system, which is exactly what happens in an unhealthy body.

On top of this, since the rules governing global trade were advanced under the guidance of the United Nations in the 1990s, global corporations now have greater legal power than individual humans. We all know how hard it is for individual citizens to take on the big companies with their massive armies of highly paid lawyers.

The Scope of Evolutionary Relationships

This is just the fine skim across the surface of what has been revealed to me through engaging an intimate journey with cancer. However, such engagement is not limited to cancer. It can be applied to any energy, situation, or institution. One could equally engage in an intimate journey with the global market, the US military, the oil companies, the crisis in Syria, climate change, the European refugee crisis, or any other situation.

When we do this we actually leverage our personal transformation in powerful ways. No longer are we dealing simply with the information fields that support our personal lives, we are engaging the information fields that influence the way our collective civilization manifests.

By truly engaging these energies in a deeply intimate manner we create the capacity to influence the way they manifest in the future. We can demonstrate, through our relationship, new ways for this information to manifest in society. And this, my friends, has the power to shift the course we are currently pursuing, ushering in a new story for humanity.

Alistair Smith was drawn into this incarnation to live the journey that structure has to undertake if it is to be able to surrender into a loving relationship with Life in which it can operate in service to the great evolutionary impulse coming from the heart of creation. Cancer has been his most profound teacher, taking him to deeper levels of surrender. He shares his journey through writing from his home in Australia.

The Courage to Be… Me

Keri S. Smith

I STRUGGLE WITH FULL SELF-EXPRESSION. I often suppress certain parts of my personality because it appears to make life easier, success more frequent, and acceptance more accessible, particularly in professional circles. This wears on me, and as I strive to be a great leader, I often wonder about the meaning of authentic leadership. How do you successfully navigate the complexities of your own humanity and combine and channel the resulting composite effectively as a leader? *Can you effectively lead if you are not courageous enough to be your true self?*

As an adult, I have learned to mute myself. I am sometimes uncomfortable with expressing the non-standard aspects of my personality, and work on projecting a polished exterior. I continually refine the edges, hamstringing some of my uniqueness in the process. The inner me screams for release and often reminds me of those moments when I allowed myself to breathe and live from my authentic self.

I Was a Six-Year-Old Daredevil

I think back to my early life and look with fondness at that carefree girl who laughed often, took risks, loved herself, and shared her joy with others.

I was a daredevil! I remember being six years old and living in Barbados. I woke up one morning and decided that my goal for that day would be to jump out of a moving vehicle!

After school, my cousin, Julian, (aged six), my sister, Tessa, (aged four), and I were waiting to be picked up by my parents' company driver. While we waited, I shared my plans with Tessa and Julian. They were both skeptical, but I was determined that I was not going to jump alone.

Our driver picked us up in a big red van and we opened the sliding door and sat down. We were about thirty minutes from home and I spent the first twenty minutes or so of the journey cajoling, begging, and convincing Tessa and Julian to participate in my adventure. Julian finally agreed, but Tessa still hadn't committed.

As we got closer to our house, close enough that I could see the driveway gate, I started to debate whether jumping was really a good idea. With about two minutes left before we turned into the gate, I decided it was now or never. I opened the sliding door, looked down at the moving road, and jumped.

As I was rolling on the gravel road, I looked back towards the open door and was excited to see that Julian had also jumped and was similarly rolling around. Tessa stood at the edge of the door, peeking out at me and Julian, with a look of fear on her face.

Julian and I got up, marveled at our cuts and bruises, and smiled widely at each other. We were so proud of ourselves and what we had dared to accomplish. What freedom!

Children provide such great examples of courageous authenticity. They generally have an intense love of life, share their views unfiltered, and try new things, caring little about how they look during these pursuits or what society might think about their actions.

I do love adventure, and still get a rush from knowing that I accomplished something that was scary, that may have even seemed impossible at first — being afraid but doing it anyway. Yes!

So whether it was walking barefoot on hot coals with my parents at a Tony Robbins event, bungee jumping with a friend in California, skydiving with my cousin in Pennsylvania, or encouraging Julian and Tessa to jump with me from a moving vehicle in Barbados, from an early age I have embraced the challenge, excitement, mind shifts, and growth that can be gained through kicking down those boundary lines and mental chains.

Those Suffocating Boundaries

I know that boundaries are stifling, and yet as an adult I increasingly fall into accepting societal boundary lines, even adding a few of my own. Rules, protocols, prescriptions about what is acceptable manifest a rigid heaviness that weighs on a person and has them robotically performing for the acceptance of others. I frequently hear criticism from others such as:

- As a woman, you can't show too much emotion or people will think you are weak.

- Just agree with him for an easy life!

- Don't be so ambitious or aggressive – people will like you more.

- Be mindful of whom people see you associating with; it will impact your brand. Hang out with worthy people.

- If you didn't go to "X, Y, and Z" schools, you are not as good.

- If you make a mistake, you are a screw-up. (It will take you a long time to recover from that situation.)

- Don't get too creative.

Such narrow definitions of what leadership and success looks like to others frustrate me. Ugh!

Of course, some boundaries and guidelines are helpful and are clearly needed, but living a purely rule-based life with limited free-thinking and autonomy gradually washes away the essence of who you are. And with limited time spent on active self-reflection or critical thinking, it is easy to fall into this numbness as a lifestyle. You start to believe the popular view that this is what is required to fit the "professional and respectable leader" stereotype. This is what enables an easier, more non-confrontational existence and lends you credibility. This is what they reward. This is the path to success. You too often accept living in this very beige framing of the world.

Pure Beige

Vanilla ice cream, white rice, unflavored tofu and beige thoughts
Long stretches of nothingness
Covered in lazy, hiding in sleep
Close friendships with the useless inanimates

Waiting on something, dying for anything
Surrounded by the mind-numbing beige
Searching, Begging
Intervene
Infuse color
Free us from this dreary, tasteless landscape of pure beige

These self-enforced shackles chafe, and deep down I crave true freedom. My frustrations manifest in different ways. For example, there's *The Reckless Rebel*: Frustrated with being suppressed, I fight back against the rules and protocols. I do not want to be told what to do. I want no responsibilities or agenda. Leave me alone! I am in control, yet this state often ends in acts of self-sabotage.

I am sometimes *The Robot,* and go into perfunctory mode. Life is a performance and as such it is quite monotonous. There is no joy, no excitement... really nothing new under the sun. I feel no purpose. The world is bland. Sigh.

Another state I sometimes channel is *The Overthinker.* In an effort to appease and be socially appropriate, I think deeply about everything before acting. I become hesitant about simple things. I am indecisive and unsure. "Sorry" becomes a frequent crutch-word. People-pleasing dominates and I am suffused with self-doubt and hypersensitivity.

Breathe, Baby, Breathe

Of course, the power to be fully self-expressed lies within. There is no army of "they" that is controlling me and forcing me to live a restrained existence. There are plenty of moments when I allow myself to be fully free, and they are breathtaking and joyous. To embrace the nuances of myself with love, grace, and acceptance, and to have this confidence manifest in all areas of my life – what beauty... and what relief. To be emotive; to understand and accept my flaws and not take them as a measure of self-worth; to allow myself to live, learn, feel, and love without censure but with joy and courage; to live each day in freedom and complete self-acceptance – yes, *yes,* and more YES! I am woman, hear me roar!

The Raw and the Beautiful

You see her and are transfixed
She is so happy, loudly confident, and alive
Pulsating beauty
She loves life and is fiercely protective of her special ones
She flouts convention and is often bawdy

People love being around her
She makes you smile, and sometimes wish to be her
But you know that she often goes too far
She likes to shock, cross the line
She spits on the rules
And while you love her freedom of expression —find her so refreshing
You admit that not all of her movements are wise
She seems to buy into empty philosophies about what it is to be a powerful woman
Much of moral law is antiquated, restrictive, sexist
She is definitely courageous; but sometimes she pushes too much, and debases herself
No one dares to guide her, to correct her — to consider that there could be "an extreme" that is wrong
She is too darn entertaining, too much of a bright spark in this world
They love her way too much to risk killing such amazing energy
And although you know better
That much of what she does is anti-Him
You can honestly find in her a kindred spirit
That candor, the truthfulness of her being her
You also want to embrace the rawness of your humanity
To live you
The truth, no sugar
To say it, how you really want to say it
Guttural, raw, full of fire
Refusing a lukewarm existence
Living without doubt, with light in your life
And that's what you really see in her
so Raw... so Beautiful

The benefits of authenticity are far-reaching and allow me to tap in to areas of my talents and potential that I am not even completely aware of. The more I embrace my nuanced personhood and love and accept all of me, the more courageous and confident I am, the more I achieve, and the more I serve. This potent congruence inevitably impacts all aspects of life and pushes me to the next level of me. Oh, to be extraordinary!

An Example of Authentic Leadership

But how do I consistently achieve and sustain this state of authenticity? What are the steps? The principles? Can it even be done? Are there leaders I can mirror who have already achieved this?

I think that Jesus Christ serves as a great example of authentic leadership. He was an extraordinary servant-leader who lived abundantly and out loud, and was fully confident in his personhood. He lived in a highly rule-based and judgmental society. There were deep traditions regarding how to behave, whom to spend time with, who was worthy, and what leadership looked like.

Jesus consistently stayed true to his sense of self and life purpose. He embraced his multifaceted character with ease and no apologies. He was a revolutionary. He loved deeply and got angry. He flouted authority. He offended many. He partied. He had biting humor. He cried. He felt pain. He had and shared deep doubts. He served. He healed. He led. He was hated and maligned. He was loved. He changed lives. And amid all the hostility, confusion, and societal pressures about how to perform, he remained focused and transformed the world! Jesus manifested authentic leadership: the sometimes messy but beautiful and impactful combination of power, confidence, self-acceptance, vulnerability, and deep love for community. What an example!

Enough of this limited living. Freedom calls. It's our turn now. Are we ready?

Those Authenticity Building Blocks

Yes, we are ready! But how do we consistently achieve and sustain this state of authenticity? What are the steps?

I have found that several key ingredients are present whenever I am living from my authentic self, and they have helped me get back to my authentic self when I've gotten distracted or lost my way.

Ingredient One: Understanding the "Why"

A key step to authentic living is having clarity and purpose. Understanding the broader meaning of why we are here on this earth helps put day-to-day activities in perspective and guides prioritization. Who am I? What is my identity tied to? Who or what defines my self-worth? What is my compelling vision? Am I living in alignment with my purpose? I take time to refocus on the life I want to live, evaluate my current motives and actions within that context, and identify the necessary adjustments. I also think about the many souls who would give anything to have one more day above ground, and remember that life is a gift — one that I want to honor. There is meaning here. There is purpose. It is more than just the rules and busyness. There is joy to be had, and there is also responsibility and critical accountability to make the most of what has been entrusted to me.

Ingredient Two: Remembering the Blessings and to Be a Blessing

Gratitude and music are great mood-changers. When I stop and think of all that I have been blessed with, it transforms my frame of mind. No matter how awful life gets, there is always a reason to give thanks. I can walk, talk, think, see, breathe, and smell. I can laugh, feel, hear, and cry. I'm alive. Thank you, God! Remembering to be

160

thankful and acknowledge the spectrum of blessings granted to us awakens an enhanced state of being. It creates a truly positive energy that is calming and freeing and reenergizes you to powerfully create from your authentic self.

We are made for community. A key human need is to contribute to others. People need people. A quick and enjoyable path to your authentic self comes through giving. Encourage someone else. Love your neighbor as you love yourself.

Ingredient Three: Respecting the Routine

Routine is so important. It provides structure and constructive daily habits that create a stabilizing force in your life and a highly productive space. Routine also builds confidence. You show yourself that you are disciplined and able to consistently keep your word. As an added benefit, you reap the rewards from the diligent application of your empowering habits. Momentum!

Ingredient Four: Taking More Risks!

Challenge yourself. Get out of your comfort zone. Life doesn't owe you anything. Get up and just start. Exercise the muscle of challenging yourself; the character growth that comes from working through that fear is foundational and exhilarating. Grow or die. Moving out of the status quo and trying new things helps you discover more about who you truly are. Push, then push some more. Be strong and courageous!

Ingredient Five: Celebrating Yourself

Be kind to yourself. It is hard to thrive in an environment of harsh self-criticism, doubt, and negative self-talk. Make time for things that give you a sense of well-being. Nurture yourself.

Have fun. Create a space that fosters growth and self-discovery. Acknowledge your achievements. Remember the good you have done. Celebrate you! Shine!

Keri S. Smith is a senior vice-president who collaborates with executive management in Fortune 500 companies. A founding member of two global businesses, she has worked with corporate leaders, churches, youth, and women in business programs. Keri is a people-focused leader, passionate about contributing to the world. She received her BA in economics (with a minor in industrial engineering) from Smith College in Massachusetts. Born and raised in Jamaica, she now lives in New York.

https://www.facebook.com/leadwithkeri/

Transformation from Within: My Story from the Brink of Death to Rebirth

Pedro "Power" Soler

DO YOU FEEL THAT EVERYTHING HAPPENS for a reason, and that perhaps the fact you are reading this book right now is not merely a coincidence? Have you ever asked yourself if you were living your soul's true purpose? Do you wonder if you are making the contribution you know you were put on Earth to make? I never thought about these things until I experienced a profound life change. It took literally "wars" to change my entire perspective on life.

Seemingly in an instant, I found myself standing in the middle of the Persian Gulf War with my heart beating too fast, a magazine-fed carbine, a semiautomatic pistol, and other military weapons by my side. Little by little my mind started to remember. I heard explosions, guns firing, and screaming voices. Body parts and blood were everywhere. I searched myself immediately to see if I was missing any part of my body because there were too many pieces of human flesh everywhere. They were not mine, but they were from people I knew, people I was responsible for. My head hurt, I was in extreme pain, and I had blood all over me. But then it was not about "the comfort zone" — it was all about taking charge, leading, and surviving. I had to take control and lead...

The ravages of war and violence are not things that just happen. They are what occur, physically and psychologically, inside our brain when we are faced with weeks, months, and years of being in constant fear of death, experiencing super adrenaline rushes and danger. Having people shooting at you or trying to blow you up on a regular basis as well as surviving more blasts from improvised explosive devices (IED), rocket-propelled grenades (RPG), vehicle-borne improvised explosive devices (VBIED), and mortar attacks is not fun.

Imagine yourself feeling upset by things that remind you of what happened — the nightmares, vivid memories, and flashbacks of the event that make you feel like it's happening all over again. You feel emotionally cut off from others, numb, or lose interest in things you used to care about. You become depressed, thinking that you are always in danger, feeling anxious, jittery, or irritated for "no reason," experiencing a sense of panic that something bad is about to happen. You have difficulty sleeping, trouble concentrating, and have a hard time relating to and getting along with others, including family and friends.

Can you imagine yourself with traumatic brain injuries (TBI) that result in permanent neurobiological damage that can produce lifelong deficits to varying degrees? The effects of these can be profound. For many of us who have been exposed to this type of existence through our career choices, long-term rehabilitation is often necessary to maximize function and independence. The consequences of being affected by these raves can be dramatic. Changes in brain function can have intense impacts on family, job, social, and community interactions.

Imagine returning from your experience to integrate into a society that does not have any idea what you just lived through and survived. Now you see life from a different perspective, but society is not ready for a "new" you, and you are not ready for your society. What about your new emotional and physical scars, such as the ones I mentioned above? How do you cope with them? This is when the "fun" starts and you enter a new battlefield, a new life. For some of us, our society, including family and friends, can become our new enemy. Remember, our minds have a new survival experience – a different way to see things – and they start to use it to protect themselves. It is a natural psychological response to survival. Now you have to learn to turn it off. But how? You don't even know about this different way of living until it happens to you. It is not the same thing just talking about it as it is going through it on a regular basis.

What about your spouse and children? What happens physically and psychologically inside their brains when they have to face weeks and months of their own constant adrenaline rushes and fear of danger from the new you? Let me try to describe it with a word from my own experience: hell. You see, everything appears normal, but they see you in a different way and you see them from an altered perspective. You are suddenly in a different home and with people you don't even know anymore – a home full of strangers. Who told you or told them that this would happen? No one. Of course there are now so many experts on this matter that you can talk to, but they don't have any idea how it is to feel the way you feel or understand what you are talking about or what you've experienced. They don't know what it's like or how it feels to see a friend next to you blown up and see their body parts come back down to earth like a sudden shower on a rainy day. And what if you've seen this not once or twice? What about several times? Death has now become a normal experience in your everyday life.

It hurts so badly when you feel abandoned and judged, not by those you don't care about, but by those you have placed trust in. Can you relate to this?

Let me tell you a little of what happened to me and how I coped. My life changed so profoundly and things happened so fast that I didn't even notice. Why? Because it was my new normal. When we realize something is wrong, it is too late. A lot of us end up taking our own lives, becoming alcoholics or drug addicts, or even in jail.

I consumed a lot of alcohol trying to cope with such a dramatic change in my perspective on life. I lost my beautiful family and friends. I ended up in financial ruin and even became homeless for a while. I had been the perfect man with a perfect record, had the highest government security clearance, and was involved in several worldwide operations in defense of our national security. Then, suddenly, I was a disabled war veteran, and now even the government was against me. Well, at least that was what was going through my mind.

Ah, how it feels to be a totally different person. I had always been the perfect philanthropist, humanitarian, and socially conscious person, deeply concerned about the state of others, and even sacrificing myself and my lifestyle to make others happy and help them fulfill their needs. Now I found myself alone, without help. Where were my friends? Where were those who had always called me looking for help when they needed something? Now it was me who needed help, not them.

People cannot understand your pain, your struggle. At some point, you just really reach rock bottom. Yes, for the first time in my life I decided to commit suicide. I had lost everything I held dear. I had become physically and psychologically different, and I didn't even understand why. I had just been doing what I was told to do – my job.

IT HAPPENED IN A MOMENT

I decided to take my life... then I underwent a powerful experience about time and space. I felt like the whole kingdom of heaven was waiting for my decision. Time had stopped. In that instant, I stepped through a door in time into a new reality – the reality of my life, the moment when the curtain goes up and you must show the audience exactly what you are made of.

I experienced an entire movie about my whole life in my mind. My most successful and satisfying experiences showed up crystal clear. In that moment I felt I had the ultimate freedom to do with my life as I liked. I could continue to live and completely fulfill my potential, or make some smaller film version ending with me taking my own life.

I don't know from where I gathered the strength, but I said to myself, "I am not a quitter, I am a fighter!" This has been a key component of my personality as I've always seen the necessity of sacrifice, not just for my own personal self, but for achieving greater compassion and the idealism of giving and sharing for a larger goal, without expecting anything in return. I felt a relentless desire to push on, to strive for greater accomplishments for humanity. I wanted to be known not for my escape through suicide, but for my legacy as one who prevailed.

I remembered when I was a kid I used to go to a special place deep in my heart where only I could have a personal experience with God. This very special place is one where only I can enter and really be in the Presence of the Source of the Universe. From this place, I made the decision to live and to fulfill, to whatever extent, *the potential life that exists within me.* From that moment on I would speak out of love, commitment, and determination, ordering the forces of energy within me and the Universe toward a *harmony of purpose,* an *explosion of power,* an *inner combustion,* if you will; to find and live the fullest expression of my own unique nature and begin to create a wonderful life, one moment at a time, knowing that today, like tomorrow, will have its conflicts.

When there is nowhere to hide and nothing left in your soul, you are faced with two choices: to move forward and change, or give up and die. I chose to live. In order to do so, I knew things had to change – that I needed to adopt new ways of thinking and living. Three of the biggest life-altering things I started to do were *meditation, physical exercise,* and *walking more in nature* – developing a more profound appreciation for it. I found a new spark of faith, love, and light within me; a spiritual awakening that transformed me forever.

Then the Source of the Universe, God, began to send new people into my life, people who assisted me in my *healing* and contributed to my search for *life* and *spiritual growth*. One of these wonderful people was an international bestselling author, energy healer, and transformational leader. She was the one who awakened a desire in me to publish my transformational experience in *Pebbles in the Pond* and to have my own book written and published. It was no coincidence that I met this energy healer and bestselling author.

As all my hidden spiritual gifts began to emerge, I also discovered that divine help sometimes shows up in our lives when we least expect it and in ways that can challenge us to our core. When I began to seek assistance from friends and family to support me through these major life changes, I unexpectedly received the news of a job transfer opportunity to Florida, and then I met someone very special. Our relationship was so powerful. As the Divine challenged what I believed to be acceptable in my life journey, it provided me with the experience to gain greater clarity of my true purpose and my true soul journey.

And from my own transformational journey emerged the *Transformation from Within* book blueprint. My very dear friend inspired me to tell my story in greater detail and to share with the world my strategies and techniques so those who do not want to give up can find the source for mastering their emotions, body, relationships, finances, spiritual life – basically anything; to provide people with a how-to program that enables them to discover their true purpose, take control of their life, and harness the forces that will *transform* THEIR destiny. I didn't realize it at that time, but there was a divine plan that was deliberately taking me through my own *healing* and *transformation* so I could *share* this experience with others who so badly need it.

The *Transformation from Within* is built on a foundation of three key stages: surrender, discovering, and healing. Each stage helps you connect more deeply with *who you are,* taking you on a remarkably healing and uplifting personal journey within to the depths of your beingness. As you immerse yourself in the divine journey of this process, you emerge as WHO YOU ARE.

Discovering these incredibly powerful stages at the center of myself has certainly transformed my sense of the spiritual nature within me. This spiritual nature is not a belief system, it is a spiritual experience.

Today I am the founder of a holistic, new thought, transcendent teaching center, where I encourage a movement toward the synthesis of science, psychology, and mysticism. I've become an ordained metaphysical minister from a well-established, fifty-four-year-old nonprofit organization with ministries in over 120 other countries.

No matter what has happened or what is happening to you, you have a true purpose to discover. And let me tell you, *you can transcend any difficulties!* If I can do it, even with my disabilities, you can also do it. You *can* take control of your life. You *can* make a decision to fulfill the potential life that exists within you.

It is your choice!

Pedro "Power," ordained metaphysical minister and founder of the International Metaphysics Center, graduated from the University of Metaphysics at Sedona. He is also a certified metaphysical practitioner, transformational author, healer, counselor, spiritual guide, teacher, and transformational coach. Pedro's proven how-to program enables people to discover their true purpose, take control of their life, and harness the forces that will transform their destiny. His book *Transformation from Within* is planned for release in 2016. For information visit www.TransformationFromWithinBook.com.

When Enough Is Enough!

Meredith Weil

AFTER MY FATHER HAD BEEN DIAGNOSED with stage four lung cancer and given only a couple of months to live, I made the difficult decision to move back to the United States, as I'd been living in Europe for a while. So I picked up my newfound European roots and left my husband behind in order to be close to my family. He did not understand the significance of what was going on and what I was going through; at the time of my father's death, I also had to contend with going through a divorce.

Thankfully I discovered something that I thought would be just an exercise program but turned out to be something much greater, as it affected not only my body, but my mind and spirit. Yoga would become my saving grace. It is what got me through dealing with a deteriorating relationship, the pending death of a parent, family conflicts, moving back to the United States, and changing jobs. I stepped into my father's shoes, so to speak, and took over his business, but I was just a novice. I had no one to consult for guidance or ask questions; I was completely on my own. I stepped into the role of provider for my family and had to exude extraordinary strength at a very difficult time.

After growing my father's business and working long hours at a job that felt soulless and lacked meaning, I realized that I was going down the same path that my father had travelled, one that led to sickness and disease. I knew I needed to change my career, otherwise my negative emotions would continue manifesting as physical illness. My father had passed away at sixty-two. I had just entered my forties and was already plagued with a serious kidney infection, chronic UTIs, sciatica, and terrible neck and shoulder pain. If I continued down this road, would I even make it to fifty?

By now a few years had passed since my father's death. My yoga practice was inconsistent due to the demands of the business, and I knew I needed to get back into it. After much soul-searching I decided to take my yoga practice to the next level by becoming a certified teacher; to deepen my practice and heal my body from the aches and pains that dominated a lot of my headspace at the time. Sciatica and neck and shoulder pain were almost a daily battle, and yoga provided a temporary respite and solace when there was very little of either in my life.

One of the requirements of my yoga mentorship with my teacher was to keep a journal. This was the first time I had explored my feelings on paper in many years. Writing had been very therapeutic in my youth, but had been hidden from my grasp for some time.

After committing to my training and beginning the process, I once again was faced with questioning who I was and my self-worth. Who was I to think I could change careers or be a good yoga teacher, and did I really want to do this? The self-doubt that had haunted me throughout my life once again reared its ugly head.

That same night my sleep was filled with anxiety-induced dreams, including one about getting a bad haircut which is often a source of anxiety and a recurring dream theme for me. During times of duress when I felt under a lot pressure and had a lot of self-doubt about who I was on the inside, I'd often undergo an extreme hairstyle change, often with disastrous results. By doing this, my whole self-worth would then pivot on this one single negative event and its outcome, thus allowing me to avoid the pain and doubt that haunted me on the inside. Instead

172

of focusing on what lay within, I focused on my exterior appearance. It was a way to deflect the more difficult problems I faced. I could blame something physical and easily identifiable for my self-doubt instead of the harder to pinpoint spiritual dissatisfaction I felt within. I would go outside my comfort zone and get a new hairstyle, only to experience immediate regret. No matter whether there were other wonderful things going on in my life at the time, those things were immediately canceled along with any amount of gratitude that I should have had under the circumstances, such as the fact that I was alive, I could walk, I had a safe, comfortable place to live and food in my fridge, etc. But no, none of this mattered when a hair catastrophe happened to me in real life or in a dream. (It must be the Leo in me that makes me so concerned with my mane!)

This particular time the hair anxiety was different because I had had my hair cut very short to conceal the fact that it had thinned considerably due to all the stress I was under. I thought I looked less feminine, and when I looked in the mirror I did not see my face but the face of my father reflected back at me. With short hair I couldn't hide behind my tresses as I had when I had long hair. I felt I was now exposed for the whole world to see. Furthermore I saw more identification with my father's facial features and found it disturbing because what I saw (or I think I saw) was his sickness. Or maybe it was really just my own confrontation with death, dying, and aging that I faced at that time.

That evening I had reviewed a video of myself practicing yoga that my teacher made during our training so I could see and correct how I was doing the yoga poses I was learning from her. I also saw myself for the first time with the armor that I had been carrying for several years removed, trying to stay afloat in a time of grieving, not to mention trying to mend my tormented heart that had been broken not that long before by more than one man's conditional love. I saw the harm it had done to my body. One shoulder was hiked up higher than the other, and I noticed that when I thought I was standing tall

173

and straight, I actually was not. I also noticed my crooked head, which I thought had been centered properly, and an inability to straighten my arms when raised above my head. I watched this video of me doing a very simple pose called *Urdhva Hastasana* in Sanskrit, which translates to Upward Salute, with your feet parallel and arms simply raised overhead, palms facing in. I asked myself, "What has happened to me?" as I could now see how all I had been through had manifested itself in my body and posture.

I cried for the first time in a long time. It was like I was a witness to myself, standing outside my body. I finally allowed some compassion to seep into my heart for myself and for all I had been through. I realized the damage that had accumulated inside of me and how it had affected me physically. I was battle worn. I understood how I had been trying so hard to heal, yet at the same time I had been trying to escape from myself. A duality existed: the ebb and flow, from side to side, to both heal and escape from myself.

One of the guiding ethical principles of yoga I was studying and trying to apply to my life is called *ahimsa,* which loosely translated means non-violence or to not cause harm. How could I begin to practice this ethic with myself? I realized I clearly practiced this ethic with others, but why did I not give myself the same kind of respect?

I began to question whether I ever really treated myself non-violently. I knew I had been treating myself better more and more at this point in my life. I had finally carved out time for things that made me feel good and nurtured me, including yoga, massages, meditation, and time with friends. Through my yoga teacher's training and my journaling, I began to also realize how out of touch I had been with my spiritual self; instead, since the death of my father and the years preceding his death, I had been focused on my earthly "to do" list.

I asked myself if there ever was a time in my life that I had practiced a non-harming lifestyle, and realized that the time that came closest was when I had lived in Europe. I ran or walked with my dog every day, and nature was close by. I could get lost in the woods in a matter of moments. The pattern of the trees lining the dirt trails combined to a form a Zen-like state of consciousness for me. There was a sense of physical security and an intuitive sense of direction in the forests and in nature, and I always was able to find my path back home.

I missed my dog, Cooper, who had now also passed. I felt much gratitude for the time I was able to share with Cooper and all he had taught me. He opened the door to my experiencing unconditional love and gave me the ability to care for another living being without judgment, something I had never done for myself. I have always been my own harshest critic, but it was easy to forgive Cooper his mistakes. In fact, one time he chewed the heels off some brand new leather boots that I could barely afford! Even though I felt sad that they were destroyed, I could not be mad at him. He didn't know any better, and his puppy teeth just wanted something to chew on to quell the nervous energy and anxiety he had while I was away from home. I didn't see him bring my boots to their demise, and he didn't know it was wrong. He just did what came to him naturally under the circumstances.

Many times in life we make mistakes and in the process hurt another or ourselves. But instead of forgiving ourselves, we crucify ourselves for doing it. We put expectations on ourselves that we should know better, and instinctively know how to do things right even if we have not yet been guided or instructed in what to do. We are bound to make mistakes and have so-called failures. Instead of allowing these to negatively impact our self-perception, we must move forward. We owe ourselves the same kindness and consideration that we would grant others. Remember, we are all on paths of learning and must learn to listen to our inner guide, the spirit inside. Sometimes there is so much external noise that we allow the outside world to dictate who we should be, which in turn makes it difficult to be free to make the choices we need to make for ourselves. It can be a vicious circle.

I have often dealt with my negative emotions and feelings of lack of connectedness and self-doubt through self-destructive behaviors and involvement in so-called relationships. Each of them were characterized by a lack of caring, kindness, and love, as I did not feel worthy, especially since my father's death.

Yoga made me confront many of my fears and inadequacies, while at the same time it allowed me to quiet the chitter-chatter and the inner-critic voices having conversations in my mind: "You can't do that! You shouldn't do that! What will so-and-so think? You are not flexible enough... skinny enough... financially secure enough... smart enough... strong enough... good enough. Who really cares? Does anything even matter? What are you doing this for?" Finally I said to myself, "ENOUGH WITH ALL THESE NOT GOOD ENOUGHS!"

I feel sad for how I treated myself while searching for connection and in the process becoming more disconnected, but I have now begun a process of self-discovery as opposed to self-destruction. My emotional battlefield has left wounds on my physical vessel, and I hope to achieve healing from the inside out as I finally realize how fragile I had become and how my mind and body were in need of much repair on both the inside and outside. Damage to the physical body represents and acts as an outlet for what lies inside; my physical body was sending a message to my soul about the damage contained within and in need of healing.

Recently I viewed the video of my yoga practice again, and instead of being critical and judgmental of my physical limitations, I decided to practice kindness and compassion with myself – *ahimsa*. I began to appreciate that under those stressful conditions, that was the best I could do at the time with all the big changes that were occurring in my life. I had begun to practice self-care for my worn and weathered body.

The day after I made the decision to stop all the negative self-talk and treat myself more lovingly, I decided to treat myself to a massage. While lying there on the table with the masseuse working on the release of one of the many knots running down my back, I reflected on pressure and pain. When does the line get crossed from suffering to relief? This line all depends on the location of the suffering and the amount of pressure used. Self-doubt leads to self-

176

harm. I asked myself, "When I am masked in self-doubt and feelings of rejection, how do I transcend those feelings without rebellion or escapism? How do I stop the negative chatter and practice *ahimsa?* How will I transcend and transform this into feelings of self-love and not harm myself anymore?"

I have come to realize, after safely tucking the self-doubt and fears away, that I am able to make some progress by acknowledging and realizing that my self-doubt keeps me trapped and unable to do all the things I want to and fulfill my life purpose.

After reflecting on *ahimsa* today while writing this chapter, I made a promise not to be hard on myself and not to doubt that I deserve love. I have learned that if you treat yourself with loving kindness, loving kindness radiates back to you.

I accept who I am today, as I am.

Meredith Weil, B.A., J.D., believes improving the lives of others is the vehicle for improvement of our own. Through teaching yoga, her holistic coaching practice, and her own journey of overcoming self-doubt and discovering her inner wisdom, she impacts the lives of others in a positive way and assists them in their own process of self-discovery and transformation. To receive a free consultation and learn more about her upcoming events and programs, visit www. MeredithWeil.com.

Become a Contributing Author
in the Next Wave of Pebbles in the Pond:
Transforming the World One Person at a Time

If you want to share your story in the next "Wave" in this series, and believe in the powerful impact one voice (your story) can have on truly making a difference, I want to hear from you!

Ask any one of the authors in this series and they'll tell you that it's been a life-changing experience to be a contributing author to *Pebbles in the Pond*. Beyond the accomplishment of sharing your powerful story as a published author, you'll also become part of a powerful "mastermind family," or as we've come to call it — a MasterHeart.

You'll make valuable connections and life-long friendships with like-minded authors and visionaries who want to make a difference in the world through their message, work, and life.

If you're accepted as a MasterHeart member, you'll receive twelve months of guidance and coaching to help you share your story and get started as a transformational author... and leader!

If you're interested in applying for one of the twenty spots in this MasterHeart program, please email Info@ChristineKloser.com right away to be put on our VIP list. Details will be sent shortly.

I hope to have the opportunity to work with you and help you write and publish your transformational story.

Blessings,
Christine Kloser
"The Transformation Catalyst"
Award-Winning Author
Transformational Book Coach

Connect with Christine Kloser

Website
www.ChristineKloser.com

FREE *Get Your Book Done*® **Webinar**
If you want help writing your own book, visit:
www.GetYourBookDoneWebinar.com

Got a Manuscript and Need Help with Publishing?
www.TransformationBooks.com

Social Media
www.Facebook.com/christinekloser
www.Facebook.com/transformationalauthors
www.twitter.com/christinekloser

Mail
Christine Kloser Companies LLC
211 Pauline Drive #513
York, PA 17402

Phone
(800) 930-3713

Email
Info@ChristineKloser.com

About Christine Kloser

Christine Kloser is internationally recognized as a leader in the field of personal transformation, authorship, and soul-centered leadership — whose spot-on guidance transforms the lives of visionary entrepreneurs and authors around the world. Her passion is fueled by her own transformation in December of 2010 when, after much success as an entrepreneur, she found herself curled up in a ball on the floor sobbing because she had lost it all. When she let go of the last shred of stability and security in her life, she discovered her truth and the blessings began to flow.

From that place, she fearlessly (and faithfully) went on to create the most abundant, impactful, and joyous success of her life in a matter of a few short months as a pioneering leader of the Transformational Author movement. Christine knows how to flip the switch from "broke" to "blessed" and shares her wisdom through her books, award-winning email newsletter, and speaking and coaching programs.

She's been featured in the *Los Angeles Times, Entrepreneur Magazine, Atlanta Constitution-Journal, Leadership Excellence, FOX News,* Forbes.com, *Huffington Post,* and Entrepreneur.com, and is a regular columnist for the award-winning *PUBLISHED* Magazine. Her books and publications have received numerous awards including the Nautilus Book Silver Award, Pinnacle Book Award, National Best Books Award, and Apex Award for Publication Excellence.

Her greatest reward, however, is witnessing her clients as they step into their true power, tell their authentic story, become published authors... and make their difference in the world.

After living in Los Angeles, California, for fourteen years, Christine now resides in York, Pennsylvania, with her husband, David, and daughter, Janet, where they enjoy a slower-paced, more relaxed lifestyle.

Find out more about Christine's coaching services, programs, and mentoring at www.ChristineKloser.com.

Made in the USA
Charleston, SC
03 June 2016